36
42

CREATION

CREATION

CREATION

Claus Westermann

TRANSLATED BY
John J. Scullion, S.J.

SPCK
London

First published in German 1971
with the title *Schöpfung*
by Kreuz-Verlag, Stuttgart–Berlin

© The Publisher 1971

First English edition published
in Great Britain 1974 by S.P.C.K.
Holy Trinity Church
Marylebone Road
London NW1 4DU

Published in the U.S.A. by
Fortress Press, Philadelphia

74 - 75130

Printed in Great Britain by
William Clowes & Sons, Limited
London, Beccles and Colchester

SBN 281 02794 3 cloth
SBN 281 02803 6 paper

Contents

ACKNOWLEDGEMENTS

Biblical quotations from the Revised Standard Version of the Bible, copyrighted 1946, 1952, and 1957 by the Division of Christian Education of the National Council of the Churches of Christ in the United States of America, are used by permission.

Translator's Preface

The writings of Professor Claus Westermann of the University of Heidelberg are already well known in the English-speaking world. He is one of the leading Old Testament scholars of today. For over a decade now he has been preparing a commentary on the Book of Genesis for *Biblischer Kommentar, Altes Testament* (Neukirchener Verlag, Neukirchen-Vluyn). With the appearance of fascicule 10 this year, 1974, volume 1, covering the first eleven chapters, will be concluded. It comprises 800 pages of monumental scholarship and theological insight.

The present modest volume presents the conclusions of Professor Westermann's study of Genesis 1—3.

It was my good fortune to spend the winter semester of 1971–2 at Heidelberg, where Professor Westermann welcomed me to his special doctoral seminar and put at my disposal the vast bibliographies and collections of articles on Genesis which had been assembled under his direction during the years. It is a pleasure to record my gratitude to him.

It is hoped that *Creation* will open to many the richness of the theological and spiritual message of the early chapters of the Bible.

The translation of the biblical passages follows the *Revised Standard Version*, except where Professor Westermann's own version differs from it. This is always indicated.

JOHN J. SCULLION, S.J.

Jesuit Theological College,
Parkville, Melbourne.
February 1974.

Author's Preface

The purpose of this book is to stimulate anew discussion of the question, what bearing has the biblical reflection on Creator-Creation on the current inquiry into the meaning of the world of man in this new age?

This presentation must limit itself to an explanation of the Creation narratives in the first three chapters of the Bible, though it really needs to be expanded by what is said on Creation in the other parts of the Old Testament, especially in the Psalms, Isaiah 2, Job and the Wisdom literature.

I have set out the scholarly foundation of the exegesis presented here in my commentary on Genesis, *Biblischer Kommentar*, Altes Testament, I, 1, of which the first fascicule appeared in 1966 (seven* fascicules have now appeared). Further literature on all aspects of the problem can be found there.

* At the time of publication of the German edition in 1971. By the end of 1974 volume 1 consisting of 10 fascicules will be completed.

Author's Preface

Introduction

It is both remarkable and undeniable that the passages dealing with Creation and primeval time which at the high point of the Enlightenment had been dismissed as utterly outmoded, have found a hearing once more in the second phase of the technological age. When the astronauts read out the story of Creation from the first chapter of the Bible before setting off for the moon, this was neither emotion nor enthusiasm. Rather, the words of the Creation narrative were suited to the event. In this spirit they were read, in this spirit they were heard by thousands. The achievements of science and technology in the first phase of the technological age gave rise to arguments for questioning the belief in Creation. An achievement in this same area in the second phase provides the occasion for the recitation of the Creation story.

It is a fact that the Creation belief long ago faded into the background of the Church's preaching and theology. The Creation narratives of the Bible were accepted for a long time without question as accounts of an actual event. These stories, together with the first sentence of the Creed, 'Creator of heaven and earth', formed the reliable, unshakable foundations which supported all thought and talk about the beginning of the world and of man. The shaking of the foundations began with the rise of the natural sciences. They shook not only belief in the Creator, but also the picture of the world which had remained unaltered since ancient times. Inexorably the new picture of the world prevailed, and the Christian Church step by step gave up her initial opposition. But the new world-picture questioned the biblical account of the creation of the world and of man. The result was a growing wave of opposition on the part of the Enlightenment to the biblical statements on Creation, an opposition which, with all the soul-searching of the Enlightenment, brought light where darkness had been. The light of science clarified the origin and development of the world and of man, and drove out the darkness of primitive myth and clerical obscurantism. In fact, the biblical Creation accounts offered the most welcome target to enlightened and atheistic polemic, the high points being Haeckel's *World Riddle* and, in more recent times, *Universe, Earth, Man*, a publication authorized by the German Democratic Republic. The attacks of the Enlightenment, with its glorification of the natural sciences and its ridicule of the nursery tales of the biblical–ecclesiastical tradition, have now run their course, and the emotion has evaporated. The time is past, too, when the attitude of the Church in the face of these attacks was largely that of defence. This attitude had become more and more entrenched as it maintained that the Creation accounts in the Bible had nothing at all to do with scientific knowledge: they dealt only with religion and belief; the discussion was concerned with salvation. This defensive, apologetic attitude was basically determined by the other side, by the attackers. It is time to see and to acknowledge this.

From the time of Kepler, Galileo, and Copernicus right up to the formation of the Marxist materialistic ideology, the Church had no serious encounter with the all-conquering scientific explanation of the origin of the world and of man. One stood by the validity of the biblical Creation accounts and the belief in the Creator. At the same time one acknowledged more or less openly the scientific explanation of the origin of the world and of man. There was, however, no serious concern to build a bridge between the scientific explanations of the world and the biblical account of Creation. While acknowledging this, one must point out the following: in the course of the nineteenth century, and beginning with Schleiermacher, the new theology in the Evangelical Church concentrated more and more on man. There is a direct line from Schleiermacher through Harnack to the existential interpretation, which has been looking for meaning in the biblical texts in so far as they shed light on man's understanding of himself in his present situation. To speak of God the Creator and to acknowledge him as 'Creator of heaven and earth' lose all meaning in this context. And does not this line of thought follow the very same direction as the polemic of the Enlightenment which directed itself against the biblical reflection on Creation? Under the dominant influence of a theology which limits its thought and concern to the existential situation of the individual, has not this reflection on Creator-Creation become a sort of cult of the dead past?

We must go a step further: the new theology with its concentration on man bears the mark of a renewal of the Reformation theology. Nowhere, however, has it been clearly stated that everything that the Reformers said of man and of his state before God, of justification, faith, the kingdom of God, stands on the utterly unshakable foundation of its belief in Creation. It has not been noticed that when this foundation is no longer there, then the basis of all that the Reformers say of man and his relationship to God has been whisked away. In other words, once theology has imperceptibly become detached from Creator-Creation, the necessary consequence is that it must gradually become an anthropology and begin to disintegrate from within and collapse around us. Today's theology takes its point of departure from the very place where the reflection on Creator-Creation began to vanish and dissipate itself. One can be even more precise: it began where the theology and teaching of the Church took only a defensive stand against the scientific explanation of the world and of man and had no renewed, vital presentation of the biblical reflection on Creator-Creation to set against it. The process can be readily explained. When the theology and the preaching of the Church are concerned only with salvation, when God's dealing with man is limited to the forgiveness of sins or to justification, the necessary consequence is that it is only in this context that man has to deal with God and God with man. This means that God is not concerned with a worm being trodden to the earth or with the appearance of a new star in the Milky Way. And so the question must be put: what sort of God is he who does everything for the salvation of man but clearly has nothing at all to do with man in his life situation? What can be the meaning of a salvation history which has nothing at all to do with real history? Science has now stepped in as lord of the domain which man used to refer to Creation. What remains for God? This is the reason why some say 'God is dead' and why many more say 'The word "God" has no longer any meaning for me'. And so it is an illusion to try to modernize a soteriology which has been cut off from reality and to up-date it in modern jargon. This is of no help. The matter stands or falls with the question, is God concerned with the real world which surrounds us? Is he Creator or not?

We must begin where, at the break-through of the natural sciences, the Church failed, and ask what was the reason for the failure. It can only be that at the time of the condemnation of this break-through there prevailed an understanding of Creator-Creation that was both fossilized and untrue to the Bible. What was wrong? We can answer in two ways. A teaching on Creation had been constructed out of the narrative of Creation and the praise of the Creator. This meant a teaching which had laid down a seven-day Creation programme, or a definite way of conceiving things: for example, the heavens were a solid body. This was a serious misunderstanding of the biblical reflection on Creator-Creation. This reflection is presented in the form of stories; stories told from different points of view which give rise to different presentations. The biblical statements on Creation had been limited to texts which seemed to be required for the teaching on salvation (i.e., limited to Genesis 1—3); what followed in chs. 4—11 seemed without meaning for Creation.

These are but indications. But they are enough to show the attitude with which the Churches defended against the natural sciences a teaching on Creation which did not in its essential points correspond to the biblical reflection on Creator-Creation. A thorough revision has not yet won through: it is pending.

The Bible speaks of Creation in this way: the narrative says that God created the world (man) and that the response to this act was the praise of the Creator. It must be noted, however, that the Bible is not proposing an article of faith. An article such as we find at the beginning of our confession of faith would be impossible in the Old Testament. The Old Testament never speaks of belief in the Creator: there never occurs a sentence such as 'I believe the world was created by God,' and Creation or belief in Creation never occurs in the confessions of faith of the Old Testament (von Rad's 'historical Credo').

One can easily see the reason: for the man of the Old Testament it was not possible that the world could have originated in any other way. Creation was not an article of faith because there was simply no alternative. In other words, the Old Testament had a different understanding of reality from ours, inasmuch as there was no other reality than that established by God. They had no need expressly to *believe* that the world was created by God because that was a presupposition of their thinking.

This has had two consequences for the reflection on Creator-Creation which must be clarified:

1. The question, *how* did God create the world, could never have been a question of faith for the man of the Old Testament. There could be quite different opinions about this. And so the Old Testament reflection on Creator-Creation is many-sided. The process of Creation has not been and cannot be established definitively: each age can only express it in a way intelligible to itself. Consequently the Old Testament presents not one but many Creation accounts. The old approach to Genesis understood the first two chapters as a coherent account which related first the creation of the world and man (1.1—2.4a) and then a still more detailed account of the creation of man (2.4b–24). The historical-critical examination of the Old Testament discovered that the two accounts, 1.1—2.4a and 2.4b–24 (together with ch. 3) belonged to two different sources, the latter to the older source, J,

(Yahwist, tenth–ninth centuries B.C.) and the former to the later source, P, (Priestly Code, sixth–fifth centuries B.C.). This was the first step in scholarly inquiry into the reflection on Creator-Creation in the Old Testament. This separation of the two Creation accounts into two literary sources is one of the most important and most assured results of the literary–critical examination of the Old Testament. It was established that ancient Israel spoke of Creation in different ways at different times. The Old Testament knew no definitive teaching on Creation. The reflection on the Creation could vary. The most striking difference between the two presentations is that the older account describes the way in which God created in a manner quite different from the later account. In the old account there is God's action, the forming of the man from clay and of the woman from the rib of the man; in the later account, Creation is by the word: he spoke and so it happened. But the investigation of the Creation texts did not end there. Literary–critical research was taken a step further by the study of the history of tradition. It was recognized that the texts which have come down to us have had a long oral tradition, and that the written sources where we meet these traditions are the final stage of a long process of tradition which must itself be examined.

The approach of the reflection on Creator-Creation changes notably in the Old Testament. It is now recognized that in Israel there were not just two accounts of Creation, an older 2.4b–24 and a later 1.1—2.4a, but a long series extending through the whole history of the tradition. There were successively and side by side several presentations of the story of Creation in ever new forms. The Creation account in Genesis 1.1—2.4a was not the work of one author in the sense that this author wrote the whole story as an original composition. The author was one in a long chain of successors; he was at the same time one who received tradition and one who shaped what he received into a new form. The construction of the narrative of ch. 1 clearly betrays a prehistory. In this presentation of Creation by the word an older presentation has been resumed in which the Creator did not speak, but acted. An older account of Creation by action is to be recognized behind the later account of Creation by word. And the earlier Creation account bears even less the marks of one single mould. It too grew out of a long prehistory, traces of which can be recognized.

We are not however restricted to the first three chapters of the Bible in our examination of this prehistory. There is a whole series of passages from other parts of the Old Testament, especially from the Psalms, Job, 2 Isaiah, and the Wisdom literature, which enable us to reconstruct the history of the tradition of the reflection on Creator-Creation, uncovering a variety of possibilities and a wealth of presentations and arrangements.

2. The second consequence extends even further the circle of the reflection on Creator-Creation. Because it was not properly speaking a question of belief peculiar to Israel, there could be no definitive separation of the world in which she lived from the surrounding world, and from the world which preceded her. There are always, of course, differences in the way in which the Creator is spoken of. But Israel was always conscious that in its reflection on Creator-Creation it was united with its surrounding world. All peoples who bordered on Israel, and of whom Israel had knowledge, shared the common conviction that man must be understood as a creature of God and the world as a creature of the divine.

A clarification is required in the face of our present-day situation. In recent times it is precisely the belief in Creation that has become the object of the sharpest polarization. Atheistic and anti-Christian propaganda has always made the belief in Creation the object of its attack. The denial of God was and is the denial of the Creator which accompanies the explanation that the natural sciences give of the origin of man and the world. It is the biblical formulation therefore that became the decisive point of dispute; and this should never have been, inasmuch as on this very point the people of God were essentially at one with other people. The tradition of the Christian Church can take little credit here. It is neither necessary nor correct from the biblical viewpoint to concentrate the conflict on this area. That such has happened is partly due to an erroneous development within the Church and Christian theology.

The biblical reflection on Creator-Creation is recognizably and in many ways related to the reflection on Creator-Creation in the world which surrounded and preceded Israel. When we examine these relationships we must again distinguish two stages which correspond to the two stages in the growth of the biblical reflection on Creator-Creation.

1. The acknowledged fact that not only the Bible but the whole world had something to say on Creator-Creation, on the making of the world and of man, scarcely concerned Christian theology and the exegesis of the biblical texts. There was, however, an explanation that seemed to account quite adequately for this lack of concern. From Romans 1.18–20 one concluded to a primitive revelation which, broadly speaking, was distorted and veiled among the pagans, but of which traces remained. It was because of this primitive revelation that one explained a knowledge of Creation among the peoples of the earth, albeit distorted and corrupt, but the situation was changed when writings were discovered, in the lands surrounding ancient Israel, which bore a striking resemblance to the biblical Creation and Flood stories. The Babylonian cuneiform texts which were found towards the end of the last century raised the question of the relationship between the biblical and Babylonian writings, of their interdependence, of their relative age. And so arose the long-standing dispute which reached its climax in the Babel–Bible controversy. The result was to concede that a dependence of the Babylonian texts on the biblical texts was impossible, while a dependence of biblical on Babylonian texts was possible or probable. As a result of this concession many exegetes became entrenched in a certain defensive attitude, striving to demonstrate the spiritual and theo-

logical superiority of the biblical texts without being aware of the real problem which had been thrown up, namely, that to appraise the biblical texts by comparison with the non-biblical texts is really to renounce the unique importance of the biblical texts.

2. The extra-biblical Creation stories had now to be examined further. In the first stage, the extra-biblical parallels had only been cited when they imposed themselves and just could not be overlooked. On the whole, comparison had been restricted to individual texts, so that usually a biblical excerpt was set beside a non-biblical excerpt. But this method was soon seen to be insufficient. Serious misunderstandings and false conclusions can only be avoided by going on to study and understand the extra-biblical texts not in isolation, but in and out of their own immediate and broader contexts, just as is done with the biblical texts.

It was here that research in the history of religion, oriental studies, and mythology came to the aid of biblical scholarship in a quite surprising way. It was discovered that the texts which had been compared with the biblical Creation accounts were themselves part of a long and varied tradition in which Creation stories occurred in not one but many forms. One can trace a history of the Creation motif from early Sumerian through Babylonian and Assyrian right down to the later versions written in Greek. A most stimulating perspective presents itself. The study of this history of tradition, however, has only just begun. Nevertheless the state of biblical research has been changed at one stroke. The inquiry into the meaning and import of the biblical Creation story has broadened greatly. It is no longer a question of the rather limited and quite unproductive problem, what is the relationship of Genesis ch. 1 to the Babylonian epic in *Enuma Elish*, which also deals with Creation? The question is now: what is the relationship of the biblical reflection on Creation in its broadest compass to a history of reflection on Creation stretching over thousands of years, as we meet it in the succession of Sumerian, Babylonian, and Assyrian texts?

The circle must be widened even further. A striking parallel has now appeared in Egyptian temple texts from Memphis; it touches the very important matter of Creation through the word. How does one explain the occurrence of the motif of Creation through the word in both places?

But the limits of the inquiry have not yet been reached. It appears that the Creation traditions of the high cultures of the Mediterranean world have their roots in traditions still more ancient, going right back to primitive cultures. Let one example suffice for the moment: the imagery of the Creation of man out of mud or clay or dust occurs together with the motif of the life-giving breath in Sumerian and Babylonian myths just as it does in many primitive Creation narratives. How is this striking agreement explained?

The agreement is not limited to striking individual similarities. A further observation must be made: a consideration of the Creation stories in the context of the account of the origins, that is of Genesis 1—11, shows that the motifs of this narrative are distributed across the whole world. This is most striking in the motifs of the Creation and the Flood which are found in the stories of early times of peoples on all continents. It is the same with other motifs of the account of the origins, as H. Baumann has shown quite impressively in his book *Creation and Primeval Time of Man in the Mythology of the African Peoples* (1936; 1964[2]). He has set out the African myths of primitive time according to the motifs of the biblical accounts of the origins. There, too, occur the motifs of the first offence, the origin of death, the origin of civilization, fratricide, the building of a tower. With such far-reaching agreements in the motifs, the earlier explanation of historical dependence is quite inadequate. The starting point must be that the many-sided and distinctive occurrences of the same motifs of the origins, spread over the whole earth, have arisen quite independently. The conclusion is unavoidable that mankind possessed something common in the stories about primeval time. The narratives express an understanding of the world and of man which in its broad lines and in an earlier epoch was common to races, peoples, and groups throughout the whole world. However much the civilization and thought of the different groups of men have diversified in their later developments, and however broad has become the gap between the different civilizations, there is in the narratives of the primeval periods a common basis of thought and understanding which can have an even further and deeper meaning for the future of mankind. And so the question becomes more pressing: how did these narratives of primeval time arise? Do the narratives themselves allow any conclusions at all as to their origin? Are there still traces of their original meaning?

The answer is, 'yes'. It has been discovered that the story of the Flood, which is worldwide, is still received today in certain places in the context of definite rites which serve either to ward off another flood or to give protection should such occur. We know from the Babylonian Creation myth that it was recited at the New Year feast, a feast which as a whole served to commemorate the renewal of the world. These two examples show clearly that the reflection on Creator-Creation took place in the context of the primeval myths; it was the reflection of threatened man in a threatened world. The Creation myths then had the function of preserving the world and of giving security to life.

The current interpretation of the reflection on Creator-Creation must therefore be thoroughly revised. We have regarded the Creation narratives as an answer to the question 'whence?', i.e., what is the origin of the world, of man? It is an intellectual question asking after the first cause. But the history of tradition shows that the Creation narratives became intellectual problems only at a later stage. It was not the philosopher inquiring about his origins that spoke in the Creation narratives; it was man threatened by his surroundings. The background was an existential, not an intellectual problem.

Let us now make clear what this means for the modern discussion about the Creation faith. The controversy was: did the world originate just as the Bible and the Church say it did, or as the natural sciences say? Such a statement of the question misunderstands the biblical reflection on Creation. Both attacker and defender share the misunderstanding. There is no purpose in pursuing this controversy further. The question of the present-day meaning of Creation must be stated in an entirely new way.

The relationship of narrative and action, or, to use technical terms, of myth and ritual, uncovers the true and original meaning of the narrative of the origins. The rediscovery of the real significance of myth is a positive result of modern research into the history of religion. It can only be outlined here. The Christian West first encountered myth as stories about the gods characteristic of and developed in pagan polytheism: as such, myth was completely rejected. And since the Enlightenment myth so understood has been thought of more and more as opposed to history. Mythical presentation of an event, in contrast to a historical presentation, has been judged quite 'unhistorical'. The adjective 'mythical' has come to be used for the unreal, the unhistorical, or the untrue.

It was this aspect of myth and the mythical that came into biblical scholarship and played a special role in Rudolph Bultmann's demythologizing of the New Testament. The notion was purely negative. Myth was utterly false; it was to be overcome and dismissed. There was no inquiry into the real meaning and original function of myth. In such a radical rejection of everything mythical the question could not even arise. It is significant that this demythologizing was concerned basically with the mythical world picture as presumed in the language of the New Testament. The demythologizing programme therefore came to grips with myth only in its secondary stage, where it explained the mythology of the world and of man. It knew nothing of the primary stage.

The newly acquired understanding of myth has altered the situation. It was realized that myth had been misunderstood by setting it in opposition to history, that myth belonged originally to the context of survival, an expression therefore of one's understanding of existence, of one's understanding of the existence of the threatened-self (and this is precisely the goal at which the existential interpretation aims with its demythologizing). Reflection on Creation meant to rehearse (i.e., to repeat by narrative), in the present world and in man's dangerous situation, the beginning, when what now is came to be. Relationship with the beginning meant relationship with the basis of the world, and the repeated making present of what had happened at the beginning meant a reiteration of the reality by virtue of which the world continues to exist.

Myth must be regarded as a reflection on reality, as a presentation of what has actually happened. Such a presentation of what actually happened accorded with man's understanding of existence and of the world in the early period. To oppose myth and history in such a way that history presents what actually happened, while myth presents fiction, is utterly unhistorical. It is much more perceptive to see that in the early period of mankind it was not possible to speak of what actually happened in any other way.

The way is then cleared for an understanding of the biblical account of the origins, of the biblical reflection on the Creator-Creation. And one can understand why the Bible knows no doctrine about Creator-Creation, but only tells stories about it. Only in the narrative, only in the rehearsing, can Creation be repeatedly made present. Only in the narrating can Creation become real again. When the Creation narratives of an earlier stage of man's history are preserved in our Bible, then there is preserved with them the continuity between later epochs and generations and that earlier stage. In other words, in the Creation narratives of the Bible the history of mankind is preserved as a whole, as a continuum, as a meaningful continuity in such a way as to preserve for the future early man's understanding of reality – that is, of existence and of the world.

So the biblical reflection on Creator-Creation takes on a new meaning. The mythical stage is succeeded by one that is characterized by the ever-inquiring intellect. Out of the questioning of threatened man in a threatened world arose the question about the beginning and the end, about coming into existence and ceasing to exist. Limited man asks about and beyond his limitations, about his own and the world's coming into being. But this intellectual inquiry preserves within it the original inquiry of threatened man in his threatened existence, as he asks after the beginning as ground and support of his continuing in the present. The original inquiry about the ground and support of his existence is common to all mankind; it occurs in all races, civilizations, and religions; it belongs to man's being.

It is only in the secondary stage, when the intellectual inquiry about the 'whence' comes to the fore, that the way is gradually opened to distinguish knowledge and belief, religion and philosophy. The reflection on Creator-Creation precedes this separation, preserving within itself, still undivided, religion and science, religion and faith. The real meaning of the biblical Creation narrative and of the reflection on the primeval period (Genesis 1—11) lies in this, that in it the remembrance of mankind's history is preserved as a self-contained whole, and that present-day man experiences himself as part of mankind's history. These chapters record for the future that the decisive points of human existence are the same for all mankind; that all races, all peoples, all human groups understand themselves as men in the world in essentially the same way, and that religions, outlooks, philosophies and ideologies all go back to one beginning where they are all rooted in the same answer to the same question.

In the first eleven chapters of the Bible the inquiry about the whole is compressed out of millennia-long tradition into an inquiry about the beginning and the end, and is bound up with the question of the history of mankind which is centred in the history of God's people.

The uniqueness of the biblical reflection on Creation and the primeval period lies precisely in this bond. The first chapters of the Bible are conceived as a constituent part of the Pentateuch, of the Torah, in the middle of which is set the account of the liberation of Egypt and the encounter with God on Sinai, the foundation of Israel's history. The boldness of this conception is that the constricted history of a small people is presented as the leading, saving, preserving action of the same God who created the world and man. And so the reflection on Creation and the primeval period extends to the broadest limits of an activity of God which is experienced and witnessed by those who encounter this same God as their saviour. The path of this small people with its experience of the great deeds of God, with its drama of guilt and forgiveness, with its high points and low points, with the word of God and man's response, has its origin in God's activity towards mankind and the universe, and will sometime find its way again into the concourse of his universal action.

1

Creation as Primeval Event

A further correction is necessary to the traditional presentation of the Creation. The first three chapters of the Bible have been isolated in church tradition and in church teaching. It was not noticed that these chapters stand in a broader context in which they must be understood, namely, the account of the origins which embraces the first eleven chapters of the Bible. The origins can only be understood as a whole. The consequence of isolating the first three chapters, which deal with the creation of the world, the creation of man, the garden in which God put man, and the expulsion of man from the garden, has been that these chapters and these alone have been regarded as important and essential for the teaching of the Church. There has arisen therefore a teaching on Creation and the Fall which has replaced what the Bible really says about the origins. The other passages dealing with the origins which follow in Genesis 4—11 have consequently had scarcely any real significance in the history of the Church; they were scarcely mentioned in church teaching, in preaching or in instruction. The different value given to these two groups of texts dealing with the origins came from dogmatic theology. The doctrine of Creation and the doctrine of the Fall were basic to dogmatic theology; what the remaining chapters had to say was of no significance.

This different value given to the passages has no foundation in the text. There can be no doubt that Genesis 1—11 is meant to be a unity. The account of the origins is saying something which cannot be understood out of the whole context. If the chapters have a meaning for the teaching and preaching of the Church, then they have it only from what the account of the origins has to say as a whole.

The simple acknowledgement of this fact has incalculable consequences for the understanding of the biblical reflection on Creation. Western understanding of world and man in the early period, in the Middle Ages, and right up to the beginning of the Enlightenment, was determined by the conviction that everything essential that had to be said of the world and of man had been said in the first three chapters of the Bible, that is with the account of Creation and Fall. And so the stage was set on which the drama of the world was to be played: *everything* had been said with the narrative that God had created the world and put man in it, that man had been disobedient and fallen and now lived in a different state, the state of fallen man in a fallen creation. The next important event for the history of mankind was the suffering, death and resurrection of Christ; and the remainder of man's history was played out between the poles of Fall and Redemption. This conception of the history of man, sweeping and imposingly self-contained, dominated the whole of western culture, the relationship between Church and State, the social system, and art in all its aspects. It was only with the humanistic and scientific revolution of the Enlightenment that a new era emerged.

This imposingly self-contained understanding of the world and man is only rendered possible if its broad lines are based on Genesis 1—3 and limited to Creation and Fall. This very narrow view, that only the line from Creation to Fall and from Fall to Redemption really matters, leaves out of consideration everything else which the biblical account of the origins sets out as basic for the world and man. There is no ground for such a narrow view. The biblical account sets man and the world in a broader and more articulated perspective. Man is not only set before God; he appears from the very beginning as a social being who must work and bear the problems consequent on this state. Man's painful striving after knowledge is his from the very beginning, as is characteristic the drive to improve on his achievements in art and technology. The history of man is not seen merely from the religious aspect. Its drama is prefigured by two lines, always interacting on each other: namely, the blessing which brings increase, and the great natural catastrophes and the division of the peoples which is the source of political history. In the biblical account of the origins sin is not the narrow, individualistic notion that it has become in church tradition. It is viewed in a broader perspective. It is seen as that other limit, that inadequacy or overstepping of limits which determines the whole of human existence. Sin shows itself in many forms in all areas of human life and not merely in a personal confrontation of man and God. It is to be reckoned with in all aspects of the human community, where man is at work as well as in the world of politics. It is then a very different view of man in his world from that which has been current in the tradition of the Christian Church. It is a vista which opens up to us when we realize that the starting point of what was originally said to man and the world is not limited to the first three chapters of the Bible, but is to be found in the account of the origins as a whole. There are some passages where the effects of the separation of the second part of the account of the origins are particularly notable:

(a) The two narratives in chs. 3 and 4, both of which deal with man's perversity, and which have clearly been intended to complement each other, have been torn apart. Genesis ch. 3 had been understood as a fall of man into a sinful state; corruption had therefore set in and what followed could only be understood as a snowballing of sin. And so the intention of the narrator in these interrelated stories had been seriously misunderstood. The narrator wanted to show that the man whom God had created (ch. 2) was a man perverse and limited as much in his relationship to God (ch. 3) as in his relationship to his brother (ch. 4). The narratives complement each other. The narrator must present both disobedience towards God and crime against a brother so as to explain that limitation and perversity belong to man's state as a creature.

If the Fall is seen only in ch. 3, then there must be distortion of the biblical teaching. This severing of the connection between chs. 3 and 4 and the one-sided emphases given to ch. 3 have made a substantial contribution to the far too individualistic understanding of sin in church teaching and practice. If the narrator has deliberately used the same formulas in the two questions which God puts to the guilty parties: 'Adam, where are you?' and 'Where is Abel, your brother?', so that one echoes the other, he does it so as to acknowledge that what we call sin, what we designate as man's limitations, embraces a human perversity directed both against God and against one's brother. The narrator makes these questions correspond so as to point out that man's responsibility to God and his responsibility in community cannot be separated. There are many reasons why social involvement is so much to the fore in the Church of today: one reason is that the Church in her understanding of sin had directed herself too narrowly towards Genesis ch. 3, and had neglected, or at least not considered sufficiently, the social responsibility which is the concern of ch. 4. This can be seen quite clearly in the influence exercised by the biblical figures. Adam and Eve walk through the whole history of western thought and art right up to the song hits and jokes of today. Cain and Abel have always remained shadowy figures. Only now has any interest in them been aroused, as John Steinbeck shows in his novel *East of Eden*.

(b) The broad lines of the beginnings of human civilization are traced in a genealogy in the second part of ch. 4: agriculture (4.1), the founding of a city (4.17), the nomadic life with cattle-breeding, the working of metals, and the development of music (4.18–22). The first three chapters also have something quite basic to say about work. There is the commission given to man to subject the earth to his dominion together with the blessing linked with it (1.26–8), and the commission to cultivate and take care of the garden in which God has put man (2.15). It is here that the separation of chs. 4—11 from chs. 1—3 has disastrous consequences. Work first becomes a theme in itself in 4.17–26; the differentiation of work and progress in civilization is presented by means of a genealogy in a succession of achievements. It is only here that it becomes clear that the development of civilization as a command of God to man includes the whole problem of the division of work as well as the progress in art and technology. It is clear that a church teaching which is oriented exclusively to Genesis 1—3 must regard man's work from a static standpoint: it is enough that God has given man the commission to work the land, and with that everything theologically relevant has been said about work. Genesis 4.17–26 is never quoted in the Christian ethic of work. Yet it is precisely here that it is stated that the work which God has laid upon man is not something static; that the power of growth which belongs to the blessing is of a quite distinctive quality, determining and meaningful for man; that one cannot speak theologically about work while leaving aside the diversification of work and progress.

Because of the presupposition that both parts of ch. 4 deal with 'fallen man', a shadow has been cast over the development of civilization, over discovery and progress. They appear as something belonging to man in his fallen state and have been regarded with suspicion and as a concession to the world because they bore the mark of Cain. One can understand, then, why in church tradition there has never really been a genuine and sympathetic interest in the development and achievements of human endeavour. The Christian ethic of work has remained static and conservative: 'Grant that I may do industriously what I have to do.' Progress in science and technology was received without interest or with mistrust. This static and conservative ethic of work could prevail as long as the way of life was predominantly agricultural; but with the end of the agricultural era a complete break between the world of achievement and Christian thinking and ethic had to come. This corresponded with the great social revolutions and their ideological predilections which stood under the banner of atheism.

(c) The Flood narrative of chs. 6—9 is so closely connected with
the narratives of the Creation of the world and of man that each
can only be correctly understood with the other. The resemblance
between the end of the Flood narrative and the Creation story is
self-evident. When the Creation story says that God has created
life in the world, the implication is that he can also destroy it.
The Creator holds his creation in his hands and this is expressed
in the threat to life. The Flood narrative deals with the possibility of the destruction of life; and when at the end it comes to
God's promise never again to destroy the life which he had
created 'as long as the earth remains', then the Creation statement receives its complement in the promise of preservation, as
Luther expressed it in the *Small Catechism*, 'I believe that God
created me and all creatures . . . and still preserves me'.

When one sees Creation in close connection with preservation,
then one forestalls a rather obvious distortion of the biblical
Creation statement, namely that the reflection on Creator-
Creation is merely giving information about the origin of the
world and of man. It was under the influence of medieval
philosophy that the biblical statement on Creation gave rise to
the teaching about the first cause. But God as the first cause is
something very different from God as Creator. The correspondence between the Creation and the Flood in the account of
primeval events has a much broader meaning. The question
about the beginning evokes the question about the end, and the
question about the end cannot be left aside when one is concerned about man's totality, his every dimension, vertical and
horizontal. Man, just because he has been created, carries within
him limitation by death as an essential element of the human
state, important for the course of the narrative. The Flood
narrative also indicates quite clearly that the history of mankind
will have an end. The catastrophe at the beginning points to the
catastrophe at the end. The interlude is the time of preservation;
the preservation lasts 'as long as the earth remains'. We see here
the correspondence between primeval time and end time. In the
apocalyptic writing at the end of both the Old and New Testa-

ments there is concern with the fate of the world and of mankind just as there is in the primeval events. A meaning is thereby given to the human state of the individual as well as to mankind which embraces both beginning and end. To speak of the Creator means to speak of the whole.

The context of the account of the origins

The examples have shown that the primeval events have been presented as a coherent whole and that consequently Creation can only be understood in this context. A survey of the texts dealing with the origins should make this clear.

Gen. 1—11

1. 1—2. 4a
2. 4b—3. 24
4. 2–16
4. 17–26
5
6. 1–4
6—9
9. 20–7
10.
11. 1–9
11. 10–32

1. The connection between Creation and Flood is the clearest. The Flood story is told in the middle of the account of the origins. It ends with some phrases which recall in a quite striking way the Creation stories: Noah is blessed, mankind, saved from the flood, is blessed in him and is ordered to multiply. With the blessing certain limits are set, just as at the Creation. Creation and Flood stand in a complementary relationship to each other which can be represented thus:

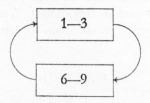

2. The creation of man concludes with the blessing: 'Be fruitful and multiply.' The blessing is realized in the succession of generations recorded in ch. 5. If Creation and Deluge belong together, as has been demonstrated, then this must show itself in a correspondence in the realization of the blessing. And this is the case. The blessing of 1.28 is realized in the genealogy of ch. 5. The realization of the blessing of 9.1 in the genealogy of ch. 10 corresponds to this. This is deliberate and is demonstrated by the fact that the genealogy of ch. 5 shows the blessing working itself out in chronological succession, and the genealogy of ch. 10 shows the blessing working itself out in territorial expansion. We can recognize now a further relationship in the construction of the account of the origins. See diagram on p. 25.

There are then two basic and characteristic forms which describe what happened in the primeval period, the enumerative form and the narrative form. The Deluge is an event; it is narrated. The succession of generations that follows the Creation and the Flood is enumerated. These two basic forms of presenting what has happened are set together in the biblical account of the origins. A happening can be described either by narrative and dramatic action, or by the mere unfolding of a succession of events, as in genealogy or in a chronicle. Behind all this is a basic cultural–historical 'given' for any presentation of history: in every happening there are two constants, the steady advance and the tension of dramatic action. It is from these that come the two modes of presentation which characterize the structure of the biblical account of the origins.

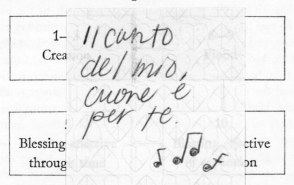

3. From the very beginning work belongs to the human condition. This is the intention of the Creator as in the act of creating he commissions man to 'fill the earth and subdue it' (1.28). Man is put into the garden and receives the commission 'to till it and keep it' (2.15). It has been shown already that this commission, given in the context of the Creation blessing, finds its realization in the account of the development and growth of human achievement in 4.17–26. This too is a genealogy, as in chs. 5 and 10; but a genealogy of a different kind. The growth of human endeavour is presented in the form of a genealogy. It is recognized that man's work is part of the growth of the human race. The dynamism of the blessing which is man's because he is a creature of God is realized in work. It is not something fixed and rigid; rather, there belongs to its very nature a process of growth which expresses itself in the diversity of the kinds of work and in the progress and accomplishments of civilization. Karl Marx's insight that the division of work and its effects are there at the

beginning of the history of civilization, and so of the history of mankind, is already set out in the biblical account of the origins. The way in which this insight was taken further shows how important was work and its meaning for those who passed on the account of the origins. Genesis 4.17–22 takes a quite positive view of the development and progress of civilization into areas of specialization. It has its origins in the power of growth which God has given. The commission to work leads to the division into the two basic ways of life, the agricultural–sedentary and the nomadic, and as a result comes the building of cities, art (musical art first), and technology. Attention is then drawn to the possibility that, because of the increase in the achievements of civilization and the progress in technology, a sense of power is attained that can lead to overstepping the limits and to mistakes. The genealogy of 4.17ff., which presents the growth of man's endeavour, ends in vv. 23–24 with the arrogant song of Lamech which suggests the coarse self-sufficiency of one whose might is in his armoury. And the narrative of the building of the tower at the end of the account of the origins (11.1–9) speaks of the possibility of a work of human hands whose summit reaches to heaven – and of the consequences of such overstepping the limits.

4. The remainder of the text belongs to a peculiar group of narratives: crime and punishment (all belong to the literary source J). The Yahwist wanted to show that man created by God is defective man. He was concerned to point out the many ways in which man could fail. There are two groups of narratives in which this happens. In the one it is the individual who shows himself defective, either in relation to God (ch. 3) or in relation to his fellow man (4.2–16); in the other it is mankind, the group, that is defective, once in transgressing the limits of race and then in transgressing the limits of technology. In both cases the defect consists in overstepping man's limitations. In both cases the human state is characterized as being-in-the-world within certain limitations which alone make possible the true human state.

In both cases one can discern a significant arrangement. The two passages which deal with the defectiveness of the individual are subordinated to the creation of *the man*; the two passages where the defectiveness is that of *men* or of *mankind* are subordinated to the Flood narrative:

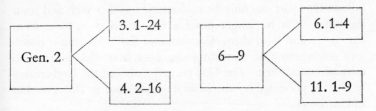

This demonstrates that the biblical account of the origins is a deliberately planned whole. One must begin with this whole so as to understand the individual units.

5. The coherence of the whole becomes even clearer when we examine the cross-pattern that binds it together:

(*a*) The structure of the genealogies forms the external framework of the eleven chapters; it proceeds in a chain of generations from Adam to Abraham.

(*b*) The creation of man is linked with the blessing just as is the saving from the flood: 1.28 corresponds almost word for word with 9.1.

(*c*) A basic motif runs through the narratives of the failures: the serpent promises man, 'You will be like God' (3.5); 6.1–4 indicates man's trespassing into the realm of God; in 11.1–9 a tower is built that is to reach up to heaven.

(*d*) The leading motif in the divine punishments is alienation from God: man is driven out of the garden (3.21–4); Cain is cursed (4.11, 16); in 11.1–9 the building that was to reach up to heaven is destroyed.

(*e*) There is a subtle but very important cross-pattern linking chs. 3 and 4. The construction of these two narratives is quite similar and this similarity is quite deliberate in the almost identical questions which God directs to the man on each occasion: 'Where are you?' and 'Where is your brother?'

This long series of correspondences shows that chs. 1—11 are conceived as a unity and so sets the path that exegesis must follow. One part can only be understood together with and from the other. It is no longer possible to cut chs. 1—3 loose from chs. 4—11 and label them 'Creation and Fall'. An almost necessary consequence of separating chs. 1—3 from chs. 4—11 is to misunderstand them. The God-created man and the God-created world are presented by the biblical authors not in chs. 1—3 but in chs. 1—11.

In conclusion a word must be said about the pre-literary and literary growth of the biblical account of the origins.

The first eleven chapters of the Bible were not composed as a literary work in the same way as Paul's letters in the New Testament or the work of the Chronicler in the Old Testament. The written draft is rather the end product of a long history of formation. Every constituent part of the account of the origins had previously had its own life-history and its own tradition-history. And during the period of oral tradition it was quite normal for each narrative to have a number of variants. When one began to establish a written text, the basic tendency was not to set down the 'primitive text', as there was no such thing among the many variants of the oral tradition, but to preserve as much as possible of the tradition. We must be prepared to find that the texts which come from the oral tradition have left traces of the many variants of that period in the final written composition. One does not expect to find in texts of this kind a unity in the sense of a plan conceived by one single mind and then followed through. The narratives in Genesis were not composed; they grew. Traces of this growth can still be recognized in the majority of them; for example, behind the arrangement handed down in the Creation story of Genesis 1 one can see a still older arrangement; the Creation story of Genesis 2—3 is artificially put together out of two narratives that were originally quite independent.

What has come down to us is not an individual narrative which has passed from the oral to the written stage of tradition. We know the narratives only from the larger works of which they constitute a part. It is primarily the great work of the Pentateuch, the first five books of the Bible, which has been composed anew out of other rather large written works. It is to these written works that the great part of exegetical labour has been devoted for about a century. The literary–critical method gave rise to great preoccupation with the separation into sources, that is the dividing up of the texts into the different literary sources.

Exegetes have come to quite firmly established conclusions, disputed by only a few, in separating the account into sources. The texts of Genesis 1—11 belong to two literary works, J and P, the Yahwistic (the German form of the divine name, Yahweh, begins with J) and the priestly writing. The latter came into existence about the fifth century B.C., the former in the tenth or ninth century. The two works were put together in such a way that P begins with the story of Creation, 1.1—2.4a and is carried forward in the three great family trees of chs. 5, 10, 11. The Flood narrative is in the middle, chs. 6—9. The Yahwistic source is inserted into P's framework so that the Creation of man follows immediately P's story of Creation. Both works come together in the middle, in the narrative of the Flood, where J and P are woven together. The genealogies in chs. 10 and 11 are partly from J and partly from P; the genealogy in ch. 5, P, corresponds to that of the J in 4.17–26. There is general correspondence between J and P in all these sections of the accounts of the origins. But J differs sharply from P where it points out the limitations of God-created man in a series of narratives of crime and punishment (Genesis 3; 4.2–16; 6.1–4; 9.20–7; 11.1–9), while P adverts to the corruption of the human race only at the beginning of the Flood narrative.

There is no difficulty then in working out two independent presentations of the primeval events, each with its own style and with many peculiarities of content. During the period of literary–critical research the goal of exegesis seemed to be reached with the division into sources and with an exact description of the peculiarities of the writings so defined. A new approach has come with the study of the history of tradition, which gives to the text as it has come down to us a quite new dimension. The purpose of this method is to search out the course which the individual traditions have taken – for example, the P Creation story – before they received the form in which they now appear in the written text, and with this exercise our view of the written works of J and P is basically changed. J and P can no longer be regarded, as the literary–critical school saw them, as writers who were original creators, nor are they mere collectors who tacked together ready-made traditions. Their personal contribution is that they are on the one hand the preservers of the old traditions, and on the other the proclaimers of a new message in a new age by inserting these traditions into, and by arranging, the whole. The significance of these works, which are of a high order in the history of religion, lies in their combining together what has been preserved from the past and what has been newly created, tradition and interpretation, obligation towards ancestral heritage, and contemporary vitality.

It is part of the vitality of these works that in both of them the events of the primeval era, and hence the Creation, which up to that time had been independent traditions, have been linked to the history of the people of Israel. So the activity of the God of Israel is extended to an activity in the history of the nations and beyond to Creation, preservation, and blessing throughout the universe. It is because of this broadening of the history of God's people that the narratives of Creation and the primeval events have retained a permanent significance. When the Psalmist sings the praise of the God whom Israel had experienced in her history as the God who liberates and saves, and this praise is extended to the lord of the history of the nations and to the Creator of everything created, it is but the same process: he who speaks of God, speaks of the whole; where God acts, his activity must embrace all.

2

The Creation of the World and
the Creation of Man—
Genesis 1.1–2.4a

(The translation follows the Revised Standard Version: an asterisk indicates those verses where it differs, thus reflecting as far as possible Professor Westermann's German version.)

1

1 In the beginning God created the heavens and the earth.
2 The earth was without form and void,
        and darkness was upon the face of the deep,
      *and the divine wind was moving over the face of the waters.
3 And God said, 'Let there be light'; and there was light.
4 And God saw that the light was good;
        and God separated the light from the darkness.
5 God called the light Day, and the darkness he called Night.
   And there was evening and there was morning, one day.

6 And God said,
        'Let there be a firmament in the midst of the waters,
        and let it separate the waters from the waters.'
7 And God made the firmament and separated the waters
      which were under the firmament from the waters which
      were above the firmament.
        And it was so.
8 And God called the firmament Heaven.
   And there was evening and there was morning, a second day.

9 And God said,
> 'Let the waters under the heavens be gathered together
>> into one place, and let the dry land appear.'

And it was so.

10 God called the dry land Earth,
> and the waters that were gathered together he called
>> Seas.

And God saw that it was good.

11 And God said,
> 'Let the earth put forth vegetation, plants yielding seed,
> and fruit trees bearing fruit in which is their seed,
> each according to its kind, upon the earth.'

And it was so.

12 The earth brought forth vegetation;
> plants yielding seed according to their own kinds,
> and trees bearing fruit in which is their seed,
> each according to its kind.

And God saw that it was good.

13 And there was evening and there was morning, a third day.

14 And God said,
> 'Let there be lights in the firmament of the heavens
> to separate the day from the night;
>> and let them be for signs and for seasons and for days
>>> and years,

15 And let them be lights in the firmament of the heavens to
give light upon the earth.'

And it was so.

16 And God made the two great lights, the greater light to rule
the day, and the lesser light to rule the night; he made the
stars also.

17 And God set them in the firmament of the heavens to give
light upon the earth,

18   to rule over the day and over the night,
> and to separate the light from the darkness.

19   And God saw that it was good.
      And there was evening and there was morning, a fourth day.

20   And God said,
            'Let the waters bring forth swarms of living creatures,
            and let birds fly above the earth across the firmament of
               the heavens.'

21   So God created the great sea monsters and every living
         creature that moves, with which the waters swarm, accord-
         ing to their kinds,
            and every winged bird according to its kind.
      And God saw that it was good.

22   And God blessed them, saying,
            'Be fruitful and multiply and fill the waters in the seas,
            and let birds multiply on the earth.'

23   And there was evening and there was morning, a fifth day.

24   And God said,
            'Let the earth bring forth living creatures according to
               their kinds:
            cattle and creeping things and beasts of the earth accord-
               ing to their kinds.'
      And it was so.

25   And God made the beasts of the earth according to their
         kinds,
            and everything that creeps upon the ground according
               to its kind.
      And God saw that it was good.

26   Then God said,
            'Let us make man in our image, after our likeness;
            and let them have dominion over the fish of the sea and
               over the birds of the air, and over the cattle, and over
               all the earth,
            and over every creeping thing that creeps upon the
               earth.'

27 So God created man in his own image, in the image of God
   he created them;
      male and female he created them.
28 And God blessed them, and God said to them,
      'Be fruitful and multiply, and fill the earth and subdue
        it;
      and have dominion over the fish of the sea and over the
        birds of the air,
      and over every living thing that moves upon the earth.'
29 And God said,
      'Behold, I have given you every plant yielding seed
      which is upon the face of all the earth,
      and every tree with seed in its fruit;
      you shall have them for food.

30 And to every beast of the earth and to every bird of the air,
      and to everything that creeps on the earth,
      everything that has the breath of life,
      I have given you every green plant for food.'
   And it was so.
31 And God saw everything that he had made, and behold, it
   was very good.
   And there was evening and there was morning, a sixth day.

   2

1 Thus the heavens and the earth were finished, and all the
   host of them.
2 And on the seventh day God finished his work which he
   had done,
      and he rested on the seventh day from all his work
      which he had done.
3 So God blessed the seventh day and hallowed it,
      because on it God rested from all his work which he
      had done in creation.
4 These are the generations of the heavens and the earth when
   they were created.

The first chapter of the Bible is one of the great pieces of world literature. All questions which have been directed to this first chapter of the Bible, all doubts as to whether what is there is 'right', all emotional explanations that it is utterly outmoded, in nowise affect the validity of what is there. When one hears this chapter read aloud and in an appropriate context, one realizes that something has been expressed that has never really been said before nor since.

The uniqueness of this prelude to the Bible can be explained up to a point. The poetic prose of the strophes brings before us with overpowering simplicity the world in its totality. It has succeeded in classical fashion in uniting together what is said of the world as a whole and what is said of its details. It speaks of the whole, 'in the beginning God created the heavens and the earth'; it speaks of the details, of sea and land, of trees and flowers, of men and animals, of sun, moon, and stars. But that would not be adequate to explain the unique effect of what is said at the beginning of the Bible. Its tremendous effect lies in this, that the sweep of the whole world in time and in space comes to a consummate expression in a work of art of the highest order: in time, in the succession of the six days of Creation reaching their goal on the seventh; in space, in the peculiar construction of the chapter which, beginning with a sentence that encompasses the whole, unfolds everything in heaven and on earth as the succession of days runs its course. The achievement in this one place in world literature of so complete a reflection on the world as a whole in both its temporal and spacial dimensions is by no means fortuitous. But one can only see this when one views this first chapter of the Bible in the context of the reflection on the world as a whole in the overall history of mankind. Reflection on the world as a whole occurs only in the reflection on Creation in the overall history of early man. In other words: the world as a whole can only be understood in the context of its coming into being. Early man confronted the world of his time in its quite incomprehensible complexity and variety. The world was a whole only through its coming into being as such; it was grasped as a totality in the reflection on Creation.

In the second era of man's progress, philosophy became the method according to which one reflected on the world as a whole. In the history of western philosophy the point of transition can be made precise: the transition from the personal creator to the principle of causality was completed by the pre-Socratics, among whom the basic elements of reflection on Creation can be clearly recognized. Christian theology combined this philosophical principle with the Bible's personal reflection on Creation. God became the first cause. In the philosophical era one could speak of the whole only in an abstract manner. The whole was understood in the context of being.

The third era began with the rise of the natural sciences. Philosophical abstraction, understanding the whole conceptually, now gives way to the concrete approach by way of experiment, practice, measurement, calculation, analysis. It is now the mathematical–scientific method that makes possible the approach to the whole.

But it is just this empirical approach to the whole that has led, necessarily and unavoidably, to the sweeping fraction and specialization in which the sciences find themselves today. It is the scientific method that makes reality as a whole accessible to modern man. But no conscientious scientist can say that he knows anything of the whole or of the approach to it. Reflection on Creation therefore automatically acquires a new significance that it has not had since the Creation narratives were living narratives.

Seen in this broad context Genesis 1 stands not at the beginning, but in the middle. Two eras precede the formation of this chapter which together are much longer than the era between the sentence 'In the beginning God created the heavens and the earth' and the first spacemen. The era which immediately preceded was that of the great religious civilizations in which the cosmogonies peculiar to each took form. In the history of civilization Genesis 1 belongs to this period, and there is nothing surprising if this chapter shows striking similarities to the Babylonian cosmogony in the epic *Enuma Elish* and to the Creation of the world by the divine word in Egypt. But behind this lies a period of primitive Creation narratives which stretch indefinitely into the past. The Creation myths of the polytheistic high cultures are still coloured in many ways by the primitive representations of Creation. A whole series of illustrations can prove that they have their origin there, as, for example, the creation of man out of clay or earth. The more recent ethnology of Malinowsky, Lévi-Strauss, and others has initiated a quite new insight into primitive thought and speech which does away with deeply-rooted prejudices and restores to primitive ways of thought and presentation the meaning they have for the history of mankind. The biblical reflection on Creation takes on a quite new aspect in this context, and thereby essential elements of early mankind's way of thinking and representing are preserved for the Church's present-day theology and preaching. This brief outline should show that the first chapter of the Bible receives its peculiar thrust from a background of development which embraces the whole history of mankind up to that middle point where it stands. This setting in the middle has a quite definite meaning: Genesis 1 is followed by philosophical–theological and scientific eras of reflection on the whole and on the origin of the world; it is preceded by the Creation narratives of the primitive cultures and the myths of the great polytheistic cultures. The presentation of Creation in Genesis 1 shows traces of the earliest of these four periods and gives at the same time the first indications of a scientific understanding of how the world came into being; while on the one hand it allows the world to arise in a succession of eras, on the other it allows inorganic and organic life to arise each in its own peculiar way.

The meaning of Creation in the New Testament receives a new dimension in this perspective. The New Testament speaks of Christ in the context of Creation. The connection between Christ and Creation is suggested in the prologue of St John's Gospel: 'In the beginning was the word, and the word was with

God . . . all things were made through him . . .' From this one has concluded to the pre-existence of Christ or the pre-existence of the *Logos*; and just because it is an expressly mythical explanation many people today cannot make it their starting point; consequently these words lose their profound meaning. But when the words are considered in the broader context indicated above, they have something very important to say about the relationship of the Old and New Testaments. These words do not point to any mythical pre-existence of Christ, but they indicate that, in a broader sense, the Old Testament reflection on Creation also belongs to the place in the middle where Christ stands. If this 'middle period' has a meaning that reaches beyond the theological meaning, a meaning that can be explained from the course of world history, from the history of thought, from the history of religion, then the New Testament message receives its historical place only before the background of the Old Testament which is its source and context.

1. Structure and characteristics of Genesis 1.1—2.4a

To understand the structure and characteristics of this text it is necessary to outline at least its pre-history. When one makes a global survey of the early Creation stories, not only of the myths of Mesopotamia and Egypt, but also of the narratives in the South Seas, Africa, and Central America, one is struck by their inexhaustible richness and variety. And the more closely one studies this wealth of Creation narratives, the clearer becomes yet another impression: the same motifs are constantly recurring, and the result of this study is that it is not true that men in all parts of the earth and across the millennia have produced an unlimited diversity of Creation stories. There are relatively few constituent threads. Before the era of the scientific explanation of the origin of the world and man, there were only four clearly defined ways of presenting Creation:

Creation through making or action.
Creation through (generation and) birth.

Creation through conflict.
Creation through word.

Creation through action belongs to the whole primitive group and is found in primitive Creation narratives everywhere. Many of these presentations are so firmly established that they persevere in the high cultures; in particular, the creation of man out of clay or earth. Creation through generation and birth, and Creation through conflict, belong to the polytheistic–mythical group; both presume a multiplicity of gods and an encounter between them: and it is precisely the two motifs which are typical of myth, love (sexual union), and conflict, that are used in this presentation of Creation.

Creation through conflict appears in classical form in the Babylonian epic *Enuma Elish*. The conflict between Marduk and Tiamat gives rise to the creation of the world out of the body of Tiamat which is hewn to pieces. This presentation was so widespread that it occurs in the metaphorical language of the Old Testament Psalms:

> Was it not thou that didst cut Rahab in pieces,
> that didst pierce the dragon? (Isa. 51.9–10).

In Genesis 1 a very faint echo of this is still recognizable in 1.2, 'and darkness was upon the face of the deep'; the word for deep, *tehom*, is a distant reminder of Tiamat, but in contrast to the Babylonian epic *Enuma Elish*, the biblical account in Genesis 1 shows no sign of conflict.

Creation through generation and birth is characteristic of Sumerian myths and Egyptian cosmogonies; it is found also in many other places. Typical of these accounts is the generation of the elements of the universe, sea, wind, and land, through successive births. It is here that Creation first appears as a series of distinct acts in successions of births corresponding to the genealogies. This way of presenting Creation is a clear reminder of Genesis 1: first, the priestly writer concludes the whole process with the words: 'these are the *toledot* [births, then origins] of the heavens and the earth'; then there is the peculiar monotonous style of the chapter with the same constantly repeated phrases which recall the style of the genealogies. Again, in the cosmogony of Memphis, creation through a succession of births is consciously separated from a creation by the word of the god. It becomes clear then that the Genesis account is closely related to the pre-history of the Creation stories outside Israel, and that it is only in the light of such a background that the uniqueness of this extraordinary account of Creation can be recognized.

This uniqueness shows itself firstly in the structure of the narrative, which presents Creation as an event covering six successive days culminating in the rest of the seventh day. There is nothing resembling this in any of the Creation narratives known to us from the ancient world. The author of the priestly account who introduced his work with this Creation story, a work which moves from Creation to the institution of the cult, has thereby given to the Creation event an orientation which makes the work of Creation, concluding with the divine repose on the seventh day, an impressive prelude to the whole piece. He has suggested the coming into existence of our world in successive epochs by his scheme of successive stages of Creation and, with the repose of the seventh day, has pointed to the continuation of this process as it moves towards a goal which transcends the works of Creation.

From the fact that the number of the works of Creation (eight) does not coincide with the number of days of Creation (six) one can recognize in the list of works an older Creation tradition which lay at the writer's disposal and which he resumed and re-shaped. The older Creation account (an account of 'acts'), which is the basis of P, joins together a series of interventions by God: God divided, vv. 4, 7, (9), God named, vv. 5, 8, 10, made, vv. 7, 16, 25, set, v. 17, created, vv. 21, 27, blessed, vv. 21, 28. P subsumes this older scheme into his own quite different presentation in which Creation comes to its fullness through the creative word; but the designation 'creation through the word' does not describe accurately what P is doing in his quite indi-

vidual way. He distributes each of the works into the component
parts of the Creation command:

> Introduction of the command: God said
>   the command: let there be
>   completion: it was so
>   judgement: God saw that it was good
>   time sequence: It was evening ... one day.

The same order of sentences recurring through the whole chapter
gives it that peculiar and effective monotony which enables it to
articulate in characteristic fashion the utter transcendence of
Creation over any other event. This literary style forestalled any
misunderstanding of the Creation account as mere information.

The same intention, namely to push the Creation event back
into the realm of the incomprehensible, emerges from a comparison of the structure of the command in the Creation chapter
with its structure in the remainder of the priestly writing. The
whole of the priestly work is permeated with the conviction that
all events have their origin in God's commanding word. At the
beginning of the Book of Exodus the liberation from Egypt
commences with God's command to Moses to confront Pharaoh.
After the revelation on Sinai the erection of the tent of the meeting begins with God's command through Moses that the people
build. The series of Creation commands differs from these in
that they have no addressees. A command without addressees
has no meaning. The Creation command which runs through
the first chapter of the Bible is beyond our understanding.

The series of works of Creation is not to be understood as a
mere summary. This becomes clear only when one takes as a
starting point the whole, of which what follows spells out the
detail. The whole is distributed into the creation of the world
seen as living space, 1.1–10, the creation of inorganic life (1.11–
19) or organic life (1.20–5), and of man (1.26–31). The creation of
the world as living space is presented in three acts of separation,
acts which are not concerned with the creation of the world
about us in all its constitutive parts, but with the world created

to be lived in by man with its basic categories of time (1.3–5) and space (1.6–10).

This is a good example of the author's method. The motif, creation by separation, was at hand to him; it is found in the Creation narratives all over the world. But it is always a special separation, often the separation of heaven and earth. P has re-shaped what he received in a quite ingenious way. In his descrip-tion of the creation of the light he has given the separation into time precedence over the separation into space and so has made possible the succession of the works of Creation in days. Then in his presentation of the creation of the world he has given precedence to the category of time, which came about by the separation of light and darkness, over the category of space, which came about by the separation of heaven and earth in the vertical direction and of sea and land in the horizontal. And so he has firmly established something quite basic for the under-standing of the world and man in the Old Testament in the context of Creation: existence in time has a priority over the existence of material things. But there is a further direct conse-quence. In the structure of the first work of Creation the judge-ment of God, that it was good, follows immediately on the sentence 'and there was light', not on the separation into light and darkness. The light is the first thing of which God says, it was good. He does not say that darkness was good. From the beginning there has been built into the very constitution of time a moment of dissimilarity which does not correspond to the time rhythm. The light was pronounced good; but the darkness, which was not pronounced good, becomes a necessary part of the order of Creation. Light can signify salvation; darkness can be associated with death. If the separation of life and darkness brings an even and continuous rhythm into Creation in its dimension of time, so the precedence of light introduces a moment of movement which is never absorbed into that rhythm. There is a clear indication in the very first words of the Creation account that the history of Creation is not characterized only by day and night, by coming into being and passing away, but that it contains within itself yet another history.

How, then, does the creation of light stand in relation to the creation of the heavenly bodies which is only reported later in vv. 14–19? P obviously presumed that his listeners knew that light came from the heavenly bodies, as v. 15 states. In the account of the creation of the heavenly bodies P repeats what had been handed down from old. His main purpose is to reject utterly the divinity of the heavenly bodies, which was a dominating factor in the astral cult of the surrounding world. From ancient times the world which surrounded Israel widely accepted the divinity of the sun and moon. P therefore had to disassociate himself expressly from this. His understanding of the Creator depended completely on the fact that in relation to the one Creator all that existed was created, creature. P then makes perfectly clear that for him the difference between Creator and Creation does not consist in the manner or fact of existence, but in function only. P cannot and does not intend to point out a difference in being; for him God is not a *summum ens*; nor could he argue from the fact that the sun and moon are matter. God is God precisely because he is Creator and that means that he is lord of all that has been created. The sun and the moon differ from God in that they have a limited function within the scheme of Creation. P therefore spells out this function formally and in detail in vv. 14–18. Each of these functions determines the creatureliness of the sun and the moon; by virtue of their functions they belong to the order of Creation.

The utter creatureliness of the heavenly bodies has never before been expressed in such revolutionary terms, as far as we know. Sun, moon, and stars, being emptied of divinity, have been reduced to component parts of a world which is basically accessible to human probing. To this extent then there is a connection between P's explanation of the 'this worldliness' of the heavenly bodies and man's landing on the moon in our generation. By way of modification: the emptying of the heavenly bodies of their divinity has been quite automatically effected where a multiplicity of gods and the astral cult have waned and have lost their power and credibility. The first chapter of the Bible makes its own peculiar contribution to the explanation of the creatureliness of the heavenly bodies precisely by emphasizing and exalting God as the Creator. It occurs only in this place.

It is essential that the plants (vv. 11–13) and the animals (vv. 20–5) are created each according to its kind. This must be seen against the background which has gone before. In the pre-mythical as well as in the mythical Creation narratives the creation of plants and of beasts was told in independent stories. A Sumerian myth, for example, tells that eight nut plants were born from the union of the god Enki and the goddess Utu, goddess of the plants. Later in the story there are a further eight plants which bring prosperity. The purpose of the story is not to explain the origin of vegetation as part of the world; it is concerned only with the meaning of certain plants for man. The creation of plants has nothing at all to do with the creation of the world. In contrast, the creation of plants and animals in Genesis 1 presumes two stages of abstraction: the plants are no longer considered in so far as they have meaning for man, but as plant-species, as vegetation; they are a constitutive part of the world fitted into the whole process of the world-creation. To this process belongs their division into kinds which follows from the notion of the plants as a whole. The interest in the plants is no longer merely functional. One recognizes rather an interest in the vegetation in its division into kinds. This explanation of the creation of plants ('let the earth bring forth . . .') is a step towards a scientific explanation of the origin of the species of plants. It should never have given rise to a conflict between the biblical reflection on the creation of the world and the scientific explanation of the origin and development of plants and animals.

Here too the scientific and objective interest remains within Creator-Creation relationship. The plant life of the earth is, by the Creator's command, an articulated whole. As long as the earth remains, there can never be a single plant among the hundreds of thousands that exist that does not belong to its own species within this whole. Just because it belongs to its kind, each individual is directed to the ordered whole, God's Creation.

Something new is added with the creation of the animals – the blessing. The creation of the animals therefore is something different from the creation of the plants and is related to the creation of man; there is an understanding of what is common to the living being; there is the notion of organic life. The act of creation, by directing itself to the living being, includes the capacity to propagate one's kind. That is the basic meaning of the word *bless*: the power to be fertile. The life of the living being, whether man or beast, clearly includes the capacity to propagate. Without it there would be no real life.

The animals too were created according to species, and the narrative again attempts to present the whole of the animal kingdom according to its broad divisions.

When one takes an overall view of the passages which speak of the creation of animals and plants, one is driven to the conclusion: the key to their understanding is a deep and lofty concern to acknowledge, compass, and present the world of *present* experience as an articulated whole in its each and every part from the very beginning of Creation. It is quite impossible to view Creation otherwise than as a whole in intimate relationship to the parts, and that from the very act of Creation. The restrained underlying theme of the praise of the Creator which one can discern in every sentence of the Creation account is not at all opposed to the interest in understanding the world in its constitutive parts, which is everywhere recognizable, or to the drive towards a complete, objective, abstract comprehension of what is; rather are the one and the other quite complementary. This presentation of Creation stems from a basic attitude which has been stimulated and driven to know and to present objectively what is known; it is a drive that will ever be circumscribed by its fixation on the Creator who created his world for this very purpose, that his creature should grasp it with his mind and plumb its depths with his queries. The passage which deals with the creation of man illustrates this even more clearly.

2. The creation of man in Genesis 1

It is clear at once that the creation of man (1.26–31) is presented differently from the preceding works of Creation. The passage is set off from what has gone before by a new introduction: 'Let us make man...' What is common to the structure of the other works of Creation is missing here. The creation of man does not appear as creation through the word. This peculiarity can of course be explained by the history of tradition: the creation of man was once an independent Creation narrative (see commentary on ch. 2); 1.26–31 goes back to an independent self-contained narrative of the creation of man which only later became part of the story of the creation of the world. Looked at in this way the passage 1.26–31 is a parallel to 2.4b–24, which also deals with the creation of man.

If one compares the older story of ch. 2 with the later story of 1.26–31, a difference appears at once: ch. 2 tells how the event happened, while 1.26–31 leaves the process of the creation of man very much in the background; not a word is said of the process, of the stuff from which man was made, of how man and woman were made. The emphasis is on what was created and for what purpose. Interest has moved to the question of what man is: the concern is with man as a creature of God, and how his status as a creature determines the meaning of his existence.

The question of the origin of man gave rise to sharp opposition between the natural sciences and faith. Which was correct: the teaching of Darwin on the origin of species or the biblical teaching on Creation? Does man take his origin from the ape, or was he created by God? This controversy is both scientifically and theologically time-conditioned. Today both sides are aware that the controversy has really lost its meaning, or is in process of doing so. When it is a question of explaining the early history of mankind or the origin of *homo sapiens*, science only comes into conflict with the biblical reflection on the creation of man where an ideological interest is at stake. Theology on its side sees ever more clearly that a basic confrontation with the results of scientific research on the early history of mankind is only demanded when church teaching remains bound to a fixed way of presenting the creation of man. The two Genesis accounts, 1.26–31 and ch. 2, show that there is no such fixed way, that a number of different presentations of Creation, which have arisen at different times and with different philosophical presuppositions, have been allowed to stand side by side. This is clearly demonstrated, for example, by the different accounts of the creation of man and woman in Genesis 1 and in Genesis 2, which will be discussed later. When, therefore, the later account of the creation of man in Genesis 1, in contrast to the much older account in ch. 2, renounces all attempts to picture the way in which the creation of man took place, but simply says that God created man; and when, further, this later account speaks no longer of the creation of two individuals, Adam and Eve, but only of the creation of mankind, the species, man; then we have a very clear indication of a gradual development towards extreme reservation with regard to how the process of creation took place. And this accords well with the intent and direction which permeate the whole priestly account, to preserve in awe the secret of Creation which is not accessible to the human mind. The way therefore is at once open to man to pursue his research into the beginnings of the human race, provided this ultimate secret is respected. When we look at what the Old Testament has to say of the creation of mankind, and do so historically – that is, taking what is said in historical order; and when we consider the gradual development which this historical perspective allows us to see, then there can be no necessary, mutually exclusive opposition between the biblical reflection on the creation of man and scientific research into the early history of mankind.

The controversy between faith and science about the origin of mankind has a special significance. In the history of human development the priestly Creation story stands midway between the eras of pre-mythical and mythical reflection on Creation (a reflection which presumes the fact of Creation), and the eras of scientific inquiry into the beginnings, which in many ways recalls Genesis 1 and to which Genesis 1 is really quite open. God's decision to create man points to man's special place in the realm of Creation. How special this place is becomes clear immediately with the first God-given quality which characterizes him: '... in our image, after our likeness.' To this is added a second quality – dominion over the rest of Creation (v. 26b).

In spelling out the details of God's decision (vv. 27-9), the author repeats with emphasis that man, male and female, is created in the image of God. There is also the blessing on mankind phrased as an imperative: 'Be fruitful and multiply, and fill the earth...' And there follows immediately on the blessing the second quality which characterizes man: '... and subdue it; and have dominion... over every living thing that moves upon the earth.' Finally, there is provision for man's nourishment which at this stage is limited to vegetable life (v. 29).

These verses sum up what it means to be a human being: man is what he is precisely as a creature of God; his creature-state determines his capability and the meaning of his existence. What man is capable of is bestowed on him by the blessing. The blessing seen as controlling the power of fertility is a gift which man shares with the animals. It is something that binds man and beast together. One cannot understand the other expressions which the Creator uses to express his decision to create man in his image if one does not realize at the same time that the animals as well as man have shared in the blessing of Creation. The blessing as a power of fertility belongs to all organic life; this they have in common, however differently man and beast may develop. The power of the blessing as the power of fertility means not only the capacity to beget, conceive, and bear, but the whole process of propagation through conception and birth, from the choice of partner right up to the care and education of the child. It is this that binds man and beast together; as long as man exists, and just because this shared possession is included in the very act of man's creation, it is considered as something thoroughly positive by the priestly writer, something promoting man's progress as man. This is what a blessing means. This animal part of human existence has, in many periods of man's history, been either undervalued or thrust aside (often together with the undervaluing of woman); it was regarded as the realm of sin and uncleanness rather than as a blessing. The 'carnal' became the sinful and the despised. There is no trace of this attitude in the Creation story.

There was a time in the history of mankind when that which bound man and beast together was seen more clearly and recognized more genuinely than in later periods. It is only now that our anthropological and psychological knowledge, and especially the results of research into behaviour patterns (Konrad Lorenz), have opened the way to a realization of the wealthy sub-stratum of relationships that exists between man and beast, and how important it is for human existence to follow them up.

It is essential for the understanding of what the Bible means by blessing to realize that the blessing embraces the very existence of man and the life of the beasts. The blessing is 'natural' to man, and man is just not 'natural' without that which links him with the rest of creatures.

But if the creation of man is set apart from the preceding acts of creation by a new and solemn introduction, then the blessing given to man must have a new and broader meaning. This consists in the special relationship of man to the world and to the other creatures. Now the other side of the relationship to the rest of Creation is stressed: '... have dominion over them', that is, over the beasts; and as for the earth, '... subdue it'.

We are confronted here with a very important biblical declaration which is especially pertinent to our generation. It must first of all be set against the background of the surrounding world. Many of the Creation stories of antiquity narrate at the same time the purpose for which man is made. In the Sumerian–Babylonian narratives man is made 'to carry the yoke of the gods'. In mythical language this means: to relieve the gods of the burden of daily drudgery. A dramatic and detailed account is given in the Atrachasis epic: a group of lesser divinities, to whom the difficult daily work had been assigned, revolts; the assembly of the gods which had been called to deal with the matter decides to create man and impose the work on him; the creation of man is then celebrated as the freeing of the gods from the yoke of work. One thinks in this context of the cult in the great temple domains where, from the earliest Sumerian times, great public business undertakings were linked with the temple and the cult. The creation of man was originally directed towards the cult under the formality of the service of the gods.

The destiny of man in the priestly Creation story is basically different. The goal of man's creation has no reference to the service of the gods and their needs and is directed to the world of men. Man is created not to minister to the gods but to civilize the earth. The meaning of this becomes clear when one remembers that the priestly account is a work which has grown out of the priestly–cultic tradition, and the goal of which is the erection of the temple in Jerusalem and the continual worship in the holy place. However, it is not the cult which gives direction to the creation of man; the determining factor is that man should rule over the earth. One explanation of this extraordinary far-sightedness could be that the author of the priestly narrative did not construct his work after the Babylonian pattern, which leads directly from the primeval events of the creation of mankind to the founding of the kingship and the temple cult; rather he plunges at once into the history of a people that came only by many stages to establish a kingship and a temple cult; and this history he presents against the broad canvas of world history, as outlined in the table of the nations in ch. 10. From the very beginning, then, man is seen in the context of the history of mankind, a context far broader than a localized and a limited cult.

But what is meant by saying that man is destined to rule over the earth? Two things must be seen together: man's dominion is described in the language used of the dominion of kings; and those subject to this dominion are in the first place the animals. Both aspects are found in Psalm 8, which is, as it were, an echo of the Genesis passage:

Yet thou hast made him little less than a God,
and dost crown him with glory and honour.
Thou hast given him dominion over the works of thy hands;
thou hast put all things under his feet,
all sheep and oxen,
and also the beasts of the field,
the birds of the air and the fish of the sea . . .
O Lord, our Lord,
how majestic is thy name in all the earth. (Psalm 8.5–9.)

The verb in the sentence '. . . fill the earth and subdue it' is used
especially of the rule of the king, e.g., 1 Kings 5.4; Ps. 110.2. It
has been demonstrated that the expression has its origin in the
court-style of Babylon and Egypt. It is formulated even more
clearly in Ps. 8. Something kingly, belonging to the realm of
royal rule, is being expressed. The domination is seen exemplified
in man's rule over the animals. The kingly quality of man consists then in his rule over the animals; and to understand this
remarkable relationship one must presume a tradition of Creation narratives reaching far back into the distant past. There is
an echo here of the ancient tradition that in the early period of
the history of mankind, the animal was man's deadly enemy, and
that man acquired his status as man in a struggle with the
animals. Dominion over the animals can be regarded as a characteristic of human existence. It is clear, however, that the subjection of the animals, as also the subjection of the earth, which is
but an extension of the former, in no wise implies exploitation.
When the Bible destines man to subdue the earth, it introduces
a new and important dimension.

The subjection of the earth has royal overtones which must be
clarified by the concept of kingship in antiquity. As lord of his
realm, the king is responsible not only for the realm; he is the
one who bears and mediates blessings for the realm entrusted to
him. Man would fail in his royal office of dominion over the
earth were he to exploit the earth's resources to the detriment of
the land, plant life, animals, rivers, and seas. Only now, when

there is a direct threat to the fertility of the land, to the purity of the air, and to the state of the water, has there been awakened the long-delayed horror at the lethal consequences of the sweeping progress of the age of technology. Only now are some beginning to learn through the mistakes which show that something has gone wrong in the process.

During the last decades, from the beginning of the era of industrialization, the churches and their preachers have often raised the objection that science and technology have gone too far in their research and effort to harness the forces of nature, that the gain in power from the splitting of the atom was an overstepping of the limits set to man.

But with such objections and warnings, apart from their having been and continuing to be ineffectual, the decisive word has not been said. What is decisive is the responsibility of man for the preservation of what has been entrusted to him; and he can show this responsibility by exercising his royal office of mediator of prosperity and well-being, like the kings of the ancient world. Scientific and technical progress cannot and must not be braked; but man's responsibility for the environment which belongs to every living being must be aroused.

The biblical Creation story here points to something that has scarcely ever been noticed. It shows, from the dominion man exercises over the animals, how he is to exercise his royal dominion over Creation. This can only mean that man, as he has developed, has learnt from his relationship with the animals. There was at one time a struggle to the death between man and beast. It ended not with the extermination of the animals, but in a life together. And it is here that man learnt what dominion is. On the one hand it meant that animals must be killed so that man can live. At the same time it meant that man entered into a new relationship with the animals, in that he tamed them, and in this relationship he expressed a new facet of his existence. The animals let themselves be guided and obeyed man's voice. There could be a relationship of trust between man and beast. Animals showed loyalty to man; they could protect, warn, and save him. Man's attitude towards the animals, then, could become the pattern of his attitude towards the world. In ruling the animals man gave personally and in depth, and was able to remain most genuinely human. But all this was lost, at least for the most part, when man in ruling the earth went on to rule the forces of nature. It is not that man's rule over the forces of nature can be the same as that over the world of living beings. Nevertheless, when man comes to rule the forces of nature, he should not forget what he has learnt from ruling the animals. There are alternatives which have fundamental significance for the future of mankind: will man exploit the forces of nature like a vandal who is quite indifferent as to what his act of destruction leaves behind, or will he, like a noble lord, conscious of his responsibility for the whole and its future, take care to see that the whole remains healthy as each new gain is made?

It is essential, for a proper understanding of the command to rule the animals, to realize that the command says indirectly: man is not created to exercise dominion over man. Man lording it over man does not belong to the original destiny of man. It can be necessary in certain circumstances, but it is not a part of that which makes up human existence. It is not in accordance with biblical reflection on man as a creature that some groups are born to dominate and others are born to serve. The Creation narrative understands dominion as something which belongs to all men and for which all are created; and this is because dominion really means lordship over the animals and the rest of Creation. The dominion of man over man does not accord with this commission.

The order to subdue the earth is joined immediately with the blessing of Creation. Increase and dominion explain the blessing; they are factors which distinguish it from the blessing which belongs to the animals. Human existence as such is blessed in all its aspects. The blessing enables man to continue from one generation to another. It is the power of the blessing that is effective in the successive generations which are set out in the genealogies of ch. 5. It is effective too in the development, division, and variety of man's works, as the genealogy of 4.17–26 shows. The power of the blessing is effective not merely in that it maintains in existence; it is a forward-thrusting, ever pregnant power of becoming. The biblical reflection on the blessing must be seen against the background of the world which surrounds Israel, where the power of fertility as such was divinized and gave rise to a variety of myths and cult. But such divinization is not possible in Genesis because the Creator alone is divine and the power of fertility which is contained in the Creator's blessing is directed entirely to man. It is the Creator who dispenses this power; and this becomes clear in the biblical account of the origins as the cyclic order, the constant circle of life and death, recedes completely before this force that enables mankind to spread in depth and breadth, in time and space. This blessing which was given at creation will in the course of history become the cultic blessing.

3. The image and likeness of God

What was said of man's dominion over other creatures must be put in the broader context of the destiny given to him in the decision to create him: 'Let us make man in our image, after our likeness.' As the details of the decision are unfolded, this is repeated and stressed: 'So God created man in his own image, in the image of God he created him.'

Before discussing the meaning of this phrase, a word must be said of its significance for the present day. The inversion of this sentence by Feuerbach, that man discovered the gods in man's image, has led in our day to a movement in both the Church and in theology that is prepared to give up speaking of God, and wants to convert theology into a critical humanism. This movement will be over much more quickly than the atheism that attacks Church and theology. It is, however, characteristic of the revolutionary situation of our day. It is a situation of utter confusion. A critical humanism that will no longer speak of God, believe in God, pray to God, is incapable of faith, precisely because with the surrender of the phrase 'the image and likeness of

God' it has surrendered the basis not only of biblical humanism, but also of universal humanism. What does the phrase mean? It is not a declaration about man, but about the creation of man. The meaning can only be understood from what has preceded the creative act. The text is making a statement about an action of God who decides to create man in his image. The meaning must come from the Creation event. What God has decided to create must stand in a relationship to him. The creation of man in God's image is directed to something happening between God and man. The Creator created a creature that corresponds to him, to whom he can speak, and who can hear him. It must be noted that man in the Creation narrative is a collective. Creation in the image of God is not concerned with an individual, but with mankind, the species, man. The meaning is that mankind is created so that something can happen between God and man. Mankind is created to stand before God.

It is amazing that so simple and obvious an explanation of the phrase, God created man in his image, has only begun to win through in very recent times. From the period of late Judaism and the fathers of the Church, the phrase has roused such a lively interest that one can scarcely control the literature. But the problem is almost always determined by a question that must necessarily lead to an incorrect understanding. It was thought that we have here a declaration about man as such, as an individual. Consequently one looked for a special quality which had been given to man as the image and likeness of God. The point was missed from the very start, that the Creation narrative was not saying anything about man as such by using the phrase in this context, but was speaking of a Creation event. Man in the image and likeness of God had been cut off from the Creation event and had become the object of an endless speculation about the alleged quality which he is supposed to have received. And this quality has always been explained in the light of the contemporary ideological viewpoint. When one glances at the history of the exegesis of the sentence (cf. *Biblischer Kommentar* I, 3, pp. 203–14), one is deeply convinced that biblical exegesis is very time-conditioned.

Irenaeus was the first to distinguish between the natural and supernatural image and likeness of God. This teaching prevailed for a long time. Philo, under the influence of Greek philosophy, saw this image and likeness in man's spiritual capabilities or his superiority. This explanation was received into the Christian Church as the natural aspect of the image and likeness. According to Augustine it consists in the powers of the soul, in memory, intellect, and love. The Protestant dogmatic theologians of the nineteenth century speak in a similar way of the image and likeness. Similar explanations are also found among modern Jewish exegetes and among Greek Orthodox theologians. The new interpreters find the explanation in man's religious–moral personal life (Schleiermacher), in personality, understanding, free-will, self-consciousness, intelligence, spiritual existence, spiritual superiority, the immortality of the soul, man's position of dominion over other creatures.

It is not without irony when the image and likeness of God is given another direction and is seen to consist in man's external appearance. H. Gunkel says: 'the first man is like God in form and appearance', and he has many followers. As a result of a thorough investigation into the meaning of the individual words P. Humbert has supported this thesis, and L. Köhler has taken it further, saying that what is meant is man's upright appearance. By 1940 J. J. Stamm sees a broadly accepted 'agreement that the external form is being designated as the essential of the image'.

But this thesis has also undergone widespread criticism. It was Th. C. Vriezen who raised a telling objection with the observation that the Old Testament in its reflection on man is not aware of any division of the corporeal and the spiritual; it speaks only of man as a whole. A great chorus of voices joined him in this. 'The image of God does not consist in something belonging to the individual; it lies rather in something not quite demonstrable which belongs to the whole of human existence' (F. K. Schumann). But even this explanation has not quite freed itself from the tendency to see the image and likeness of God as a something, a quality, even when it is explained that this something is not discernible.

A very different approach can be seen in Karl Barth: 'It consists not in something or other than man is or does. It exists just because man himself and as such exists as a creature of God. He would not be man if he were not God's image. He is God's image just because he is man' (*Kirchliche Dogmatik* III, 1, p. 206). But this quite new explanation of the image and likeness of God only becomes clear when it is explained in the context of the Creation event. Barth does just this: it really ought to be described as the 'special character of human existence by virtue of which is as it were a Thou which can be addressed by God and an I which is responsible before God' (*Kirchliche Dogmatik* III, 1, pp. 204–233). A number of interpreters of the Old Testament have expressed their agreement with Barth in this – for example, J. J. Stamm and F. Horst:

It means rather the very personal existence of man as an extraordinary grace of God, who out of his own sovereign freedom has granted to man alone of all creatures a quite unique position before him; he wanted to give man something corresponding to himself so that he could speak with him, have community with him, and man on his side should subject himself to God so as to speak with him, to stand before him, and to live and move before his face.

The latest explanation is the result of research in the field of the history of religions. It had a forerunner in the work of J. Hehn (1915) and in the works of some later scholars. W. H. Schmidt and H. Wildberger have assembled an impressive foundation for this explanation consisting of a long series of texts from Egypt and Mesopotamia in which the king is described as the image of God. Both scholars support the thesis that what is said of the king as the image of God in Egypt and Mesopotamia is the basis of the Genesis text. Their conclusion is that the image of God is to be understood in the sense of viceroy or representative (G. von Rad had already drawn attention to this in his commentary), 'man is . . . God's representative . . . there is but one legitimate image through which God shows himself in the world, and that is man' (H. Wildberger). 'When the king is said to be the image or representative of God on earth then the meaning is that the divinity appears where the king appears. According to the New Testament, then, God is proclaimed where man is. Man represents, witnesses God on earth' (W. H. Schmidt). But objections to this explanation arise at once: such an explanation of the image and likeness of God does not correspond to the overall understanding of the relationship of God and man in the priestly writing. According to the priestly tradition there can be a manifestation or proclamation or representation of God only in the context of the holy place and the holy event. God manifests himself in his glory (*kabod*), but not in man. And the view that man represents God on earth has difficulties. It is quite meaningful for the king to represent the divinity; he represents God before the people and for the people. But before whom or for whom does mankind represent God?

H. Wildberger and W. H. Schmidt have used the comparative method in their inquiry into the meaning of the phrase 'image of God'. But one must look for parallels to a Creator God who creates man according to the image of God. V. Maag has done this and has brought forward other texts in which the creation of man in the image of God is presented. He comes to the conclusion: 'Whatever one may have thought of the matter of the transfer of the divine image to the creature, it is the image of one divinity according to which man has been fashioned.' From these parallels V. Maag arrives at the same explanation of Genesis 1.26 as has already been given above as a result of the current discussion. He says, 'that the gods have created one to stand before them who corresponds to them; the divinity must create . . . one to stand before them who is like them.'

If this explanation corresponds to the text then it has far-reaching consequences. If no particular quality of man is meant, but simply being man, then this cuts through all differences between men, it cuts through all differences in religion, through all differences between believer and non-believer. It applies equally to the Hindu, the Mohammedan, the Christian, secularized man, the atheist. No human being can be excepted. Because it is directed at mankind as created by God, it applies to each and every man, independent of whether he is a believer or not. It is just as valid as the statement that all men are creatures of God; in fact what is said of the image and likeness of God is but an explication of the statement of creation. It says what being a creature means for man. Man's dignity is founded on his being a creature; God, by creating man in his own image, has given man his human dignity. The secular notion of the dignity of man has retained something of the religious right up to the present day. It is normally used only in a solemn context, and not at all in everyday speech. This cannot be otherwise because the notion retains its religious roots even in the secularized world. If one really means that dignity belongs to man as such, to the whole human race and thereby to each individual who belongs to the human race, then this can be said only from outside the ambit of the human race. How one defines this dignity more closely is a quite independent matter. When one speaks of human dignity then something vital springs from the creation declaration which is contained in the sentence that God created man according to his image. The biblical declaration about the dignity of man differs from the secular view in this, that it says something not only about human worth but also about the meaning of human existence; man – everyman – is created for this purpose: namely, that something may happen between him and God and that thereby his life may receive a meaning.

4. 'See: it was very good'

All the works of Creation in the Creation story of the priestly tradition end with the phrase: 'God saw that it was good.' And at the end, God looks at everything which he had created, 'and see, it was very good'. The sentence belongs to the whole structure of the Creation story with its divisions into the individual works of God. A work which a worker or master craftsman prepares is, from the very start, always in a certain context; it is prepared so that it is good for some purpose or for some person. 'Good' in this context does not mean some sort of objective judgement, a judgement given according to already fixed and objective standards. It is rather this: it is good or suited for the purpose for which it is being prepared; it corresponds to its goal.

But for what or for whom can creation be good? One cannot say for man, because man is a part of it. Nor can man say: for God, because God has created his work for everyone or for something. It can only mean that Creation is good for that for which God intends it. What that is has not yet been stated. The Creation story with its goal as the rest on the seventh day shows that Creation introduces a self-contained history – history in the broadest sense that can be given to the word – a history of the cosmos and in the midst of it a history of the human race which, as it has grown out of God's Creation, will also have a goal, which has been set for it by God. Looking then at the history both of the cosmos and of mankind, 'all is very good'.

What is good is good in the eyes of God: *God* looks at his work and *he* says of it that all is very good. The priestly tradition is thereby saying that this goodness in Creation is not something which man notices in the works of God; it is not a judgement which man exercises. This sentence which runs through the chapter, that the works of Creation are good, will not disappear just because in the eyes of man there is much in the works of Creation that is not good, much that is incomprehensible, much that appears savage and senseless. This sentence is pronounced despite such negative experience and judgement of the world and despite the never-ending questions after the why, after the meaning.

It is only against this background that it has meaning. One can say that it is only a continuation of the first sentence, that God is Creator. Man, then, who is a creature, is thereby deprived of passing judgement on the whole of Creation. How could a creature survey the whole of Creation, anticipate its course and pass judgement?

The Creation story now speaks of the whole in such a way that it has a context and a meaning. It has context and meaning in its origin from the Creator, and the Creator can say that it is good.

The joy of Creation is thereby opened up to man. That is the meaning of the sentence that in God's eyes all was very good. Man is freed from passing judgement on the whole, he is freed from swaying from positive to negative, he is freed from deciding for an ideological optimism or pessimism. He is freed, too, to rejoice in the fact of his creation and in his Creator without anxiety and without doubt. This sentence at the end of the Creation story, that in the eyes of God all was very good, makes possible a full, unfettered joy in the gifts of Creation, a revelling in the limitless forces given to nature, a rejoicing with the happy, and an immersion in the fullness and abundance that belong to Creation. But the sentence likewise makes possible suffering with him who suffers, the ability to withstand catastrophes, to persevere in the midst of questions after the why, simply because the goodness of what is created can be disturbed only by the Creator himself.

If the sentence about the goodness of what is created runs through the whole of the Creation narrative as if it were a response of each of the works, this is an indication that there must be a response to the works of God. Praise is already hidden in this sentence, praise which will respond to God's work in Creation and in man when the process of Creation has been completed and the history of what has been created begins. There is both hidden and hinted in the sentence what is expressed in those Psalms which call all Creation to praise:

> Praise the Lord from the heavens,
> praise him in the highest . . .
> praise him sun and moon,
> praise him, all you shining stars . . .

praise the Lord from the earth,
you sea monsters and all deeps,
fire and hail, snow and frost, ...
beasts and all cattle, ...
young men and maidens together,
old men and children ... (Ps. 148).

What does this mean? Clearly what is proper to each and every
creature does not consist in its material and specific existence,
but in its relationship, in its belonging to a whole, in its position
before its Creator. It can only mean that everything that is shares
in the whole in a way that is not completely demonstrable. But
it is there from its very origin, an origin which is also ours. And
it is just this that is expressed by the word 'praise'. There is
nothing which is not capable of praising its Creator; this capacity
of directing one's being to the Creator is shared by man and by
all creatures. Praise is joy in a to-God-directed existence, and this
joy in existence belongs to Creation as a whole.

The Hebrew word *tob*, which we translate by 'good', has a
broader area of meaning than our 'good'. It can also include our
word 'beautiful'. We can hear in this sentence the overtone:
'...and see, it was very beautiful.' It must be remarked, however, that the Old Testament has a basically different understanding of the beautiful than is current among us. Our understanding
is strongly coloured by the Greek understanding where the
beautiful is primarily a being. In the Old Testament the beautiful is primarily an event; the proper approach to the beautiful is
in this context not the beholding of something which is there, an
image or perhaps a statue, but the encounter. The beautiful is
experience in the encounter. This is true of beauty both in regard
to man and in regard to what has been created (see below the
remarks on 2.23). One must understand that the pictorial art
played no role in ancient Israel ('thou shalt not make for thyself
any image'), but all art was realized in vocal art and in the art
of speech.

It must also be realized that in Israel the peculiar, typical reaction to a confrontation with something beautiful was not contemplation nor beholding nor, least of all, passing judgement; it was rather joy expressing itself in speech; and that is precisely what is meant by praise. It is in praise that the beauty of Creation is grasped:

> O Lord my God, thou art very great!
> Thou art clothed with honour and majesty,
> O coverest thyself with light as with a garment, . . .
> Thou makest springs gush forth in the valleys;
> they flow between the hills,
> they give drink to every beast of the field;
> the wild asses quench their thirst.
> By them the birds of the air have their habitation;
> they sing among the branches (Ps. 104).

Such existential joy bursting into articulate praise and such joy in what is created is, in the Old Testament, the perfectly natural effect of the knowledge that this world has its origin in the good will and work of the Creator, and that the existence of man in all its aspects is founded in the same. Because everything that God created was good, the history of the cosmos and of mankind has been given an indestructible meaning, inasmuch as it is something good in the eyes of God.

5. God's rest

The tradition which lies behind the verses which conclude the work of Creation (2.1–3) is the motive widely spread in early Creation narratives of the *otiositas* (rest, inactivity) of the Creator God after the work of Creation. 'It is in a certain sense the completion of his creative work' (R. Pettazzoni). The Creator may no more step into the work which he has completed; he may no more disturb the order which has been established. P has modified this old motif by uniting it with the idea of the seven days of work. What is special to the seventh day was already part of this motif. The works of Creation are fitted into an overall time scheme, part of which is the procession of the days of work into a day of rest. The sanctification of the seventh day forms part of the time established with Creation: the days of work have their goal in a day which is different from them. There is more here than a reference to the Sabbath as it was later instituted in Israel. There is an order established for mankind according to which time is divided into the everyday and the special, and the everyday reaches its goal in the special. The work of Creation which began with the division of light from darkness ends with yet another division. The very existence of *all* that has been created is determined by the polarity of night and day. God has built into the succession of ordinary days a movement which is a gift to the creature which has been created in his image. The ordinary days flow into a special day. The course of human history which was set in motion with the conclusion of Creation by the sanctification of the seventh day is no longer a monotonous succession in the monotonous rhythm of life; it runs to its goal just like the days of the week. What is peculiar to the holy day in the course of everyday happenings is that it points to the goal of the creature which God has created in his image. The work which has been laid upon man is not his goal. His goal is the eternal rest which has been suggested in the rest of the seventh day.

3

The Creation and Limits of Man
in Genesis 2–3

(An asterisk indicates where the translation differs from that of the
Revised Standard Version.)

2

4b *When the Lord God made the earth and the heavens –
5   *there was not yet plant of the field on the earth
            nor had any shrub yet sprung up,
        for the Lord God had not yet caused it to rain upon the
        earth,
            nor was there any man to till the ground;
6 *and a flood used rise from the earth
            and water the whole face of the ground –
7 then the Lord God formed man of dust from the ground,
            and breathed into his nostrils the breath of life;
    and man became a living being.

8 And the Lord God planted a garden in Eden, in the east;
            and there he put the man whom he had formed.
9 And out of the ground the Lord God made to grow every
    tree
            that is pleasant to the sight and good for food,
            the tree of life also in the midst of the garden,
            and the tree of the knowledge of good and evil.

10 A river flowed out of Eden to water the garden,
            and there it divided and became four rivers.

11 The name of the first is Pishon; it is the one that flows
around the whole land of Havilah, where there is gold;

12   and the gold of that land is good;
    bdellium and onyx stone are there.

13 The name of the second river is Gihon;
    it is the one which flows around the whole land of Cush.

14 And the name of the third river is Tigris, which flows east
of Assyria.
    And the fourth river is the Euphrates.

15 The Lord God took the man and put him in the garden of
Eden
    to till it and keep it.

16 And the Lord God commanded the man, saying,
    'You may freely eat of every tree of the garden;

17   but of the tree of the knowledge of good and evil you
shall not eat,
    for in the day that you eat of it you shall die.

18 Then the Lord God said,
    'It is not good that the man should be alone;
    I will make him a helper fit for him.'

19 So out of the ground the Lord God formed every beast of
the field
    and every bird of the air,
    and brought them to the man to see what he would call
them;
    and whatever the man called every living creature, that
was its name.

20 The man gave names to all cattle, and to the birds of the air,
    and to every beast of the field;
    but for the man there was not found a helper fit for him.

21 So the Lord God caused a deep sleep to fall upon the man,
    and while he slept took one of his ribs and closed up its
place with flesh;

22 and the rib which the Lord God had taken from the man he made into a woman and brought her to the man.

23 Then the man said,

'This at last is bone of my bones and flesh of my flesh;
she shall be called Woman, because she was taken out of Man.'

24 Therefore a man leaves his father and his mother and cleaves to his wife,

and they become one flesh.

25 *And the man and his wife were both naked,

and they felt no shame towards each other.

3

1 Now the serpent was more subtle than any other wild creature that the Lord God had made.

He said to the woman, 'Did God say,

"You shall not eat of any tree of the garden?" '

2 And the woman said to the serpent,

'We may eat of the fruit of the trees of the garden;

3 but God said, "You shall not eat of the fruit of the tree which is in the midst of the garden,

neither shall you touch it, lest you die." '

4 But the serpent said to the woman,

'You will not die.

5 For God knows that when you eat of it your eyes will be opened,

and you will be like God, knowing good and evil.'

6 So when the woman saw that the tree was good for food,

and that it was a delight to the eyes,
and that the tree was to be desired to make one wise,
she took of its fruit and ate;
and she also gave some to her husband, and he ate.

7 Then the eyes of both were opened, and they knew that they were naked;

and they sewed fig leaves together and made themselves aprons.

8 *When they heard the sound of the Lord God,
         moving in the garden in the cool of the day,
         then the man and his wife hid themselves from the presence of the Lord God among the trees of the garden.

9 But the Lord God called to the man, and said to him, 'Where are you?'

10 And he said, 'I heard the sound of thee in the garden, and I was afraid, because I was naked; and I hid myself.'

11 He said, 'Who told you that you were naked?
         Have you eaten of the tree of which I commanded you not to eat?'

12 The man said, 'The woman whom thou gavest to be with me,
         she gave me fruit of the tree, and I ate.'

13 Then the Lord God said to the woman,
         'What is this that you have done?'
    The woman said, 'The serpent beguiled me, and I ate.'

14 The Lord God said to the serpent,
         'Because you have done this,
             cursed are you above all cattle,
             and above all wild animals;
         upon your belly you shall go,
             and dust you shall eat all the days of your life.

15 *I am putting enmity between you and the woman,
         between her seed and your seed;
         he will crush your head and you will snap at his heel.'

16 To the woman he said,
    'I will greatly multiply your pain in childbearing;
         in pain you shall bring forth children,
         yet your desire shall be for your husband, and he shall rule over you.'

17 *And to the man he said,

> 'Because you have listened to the voice of your wife,
> and have eaten of the tree of which I commanded you,
> "You shall not eat of it,"
> cursed is the ground because of you;
> in toil you shall eat of it all the days of your life;

18 thorns and thistles it shall bring forth to you;
> and you shall eat the plants of the field.

19 In the sweat of your face you shall eat bread,
> till you return to the ground,
> for out of it you were taken;
> you are dust, and to dust you shall return.'

20 The man called his wife's name Eve,
> because she was the mother of all living.

21 *And the Lord God made for the man and for his wife garments of skins, and clothed them.

22 Then the Lord God said,

> 'Behold, the man has become like one of us,
> knowing good and evil;
> and now, lest he put forth his hand and take also of the tree of life,
> and live for ever' —

23 therefore the Lord God sent him forth from the garden of Eden,
> to till the ground from which he was taken.

24 He drove out the man;
> and at the east of the garden of Eden he placed cherubim,
> and a flaming sword which turned every way,
> to guard the way to the tree of life.

1. Creation of the world and creation of man

Stories of the creation of the world and of man have an impressive prehistory. They have their origin not in the high cultures of the Near East, east Asia and Central America, but in the primitive cultures of all continents; they stretch as far back into prehistory as does the witness of oral tradition. It has been recognized only recently that stories of the creation of the world and of the creation of man are not originally connected; they once represented independent traditions. And it can be shown that the narrative of the creation of man is older than that of the creation of the world. The present state of our knowledge tells us that the stories of the creation of the world were formed first in the high cultures, while the stories of the creation of man everywhere stretch right back into the primitive cultures. A striking proof of this is that in Egyptian mythology the cosmogony, the creation of the world, is the dominant theme in the Creation stories, while in the rest of Africa, south of the Equator, the stories of the creation of man are highly developed, but those of the creation of the world scarcely exist and, when they do, they appear only by way of additions.

The idea of creation, of origin, arose then in the context of the creation of man. Before man looked at the world as a whole and was able to stand off and ask how it came to be, he had already come to a global understanding of his own existence so that he was able to ask how he came to be and to tell stories about the origin of man. This questioning did not arise out of any theoretical interest, but out of a state of human existence seen as threatened. The conclusion is that the question about existence is older than the question about the one who exists. Theology and philosophy, knowledge and faith, are not distinguished from each other in this inquiry about human existence which the stories of the creation of man present. The Creation narratives arose before these distinctions were made. They express an understanding of human existence which was once meaningful but which is no longer comprehensible to us. They deal with the very basis of existence. And so we come to realize that these stories about the creation of man were handed down in a fixed form which we have difficulty in grasping. The themes of the Creation stories have persevered through tens of thousands of years and the distribution of certain Creation themes over the whole

world – for example, the creation of man out of mud or clay together with the breathing in of the breath of life – still defies any
explanation. When we read the biblical stories of the creation of
man in our own language, we read first of all the final form of
an address to his contemporaries of an author and theologian of
the Israelite people in the tenth century before Christ. We read
at the same time something that stretches beyond this masterpiece into the far distant past.

2. The narrative

The prehistory can be discerned in two originally independent
stories which even now can be easily separated from each other,
but which have been so smoothly blended together that the result
is a perfectly self-contained narrative. One tells how God put man
into the garden, provided him with plenty of nourishment, and
forbade him to eat the fruit of one of the trees in the garden
under the penalty of death. Man was led astray by the serpent
and ate of the fruit of this tree. God discovered the violation of
his commandment and punished man by driving him out of the
garden. The other narrative is one of many which deal with the
creation of man. It tells how at the beginning God formed man
from the earth and breathed into him the breath of life, but then
noticed that his creature was not yet complete. God tried to make
up for what was lacking by the creation of the animals; but they
were not adequate. God then created woman out of man's rib
and man welcomed her with joy. Only when man and woman
are there together is the creation of mankind accomplished.

The Yahwist, by blending these two narratives into one, has
brought together in one sweep the creation of man and man's
first defection. He has made it clear from the start that we cannot speak of one without at the same time thinking of the other.
Man is from God's point of view 'adequate'; he has been created
good, but it is of the very essence of man, inseparable from his
nature, that he is defective. He is such that he can rise up against
his Creator and be disobedient to him. From his beginning man
appears in a state of conflict: God has given him his being, yet

he can set himself up against God. Man is only man in the midst of this conflict.

The Yahwist has introduced yet another motif into his carefully woven narrative. He has chosen a Creation story which is directed at man in community. Man as a lone individual, so the narrative runs, is not yet the creature which God intended. Man is only really man in the I–thou relationship. In this way the Yahwist shows that man's offence, his disobedience towards God, is not the act of an individual, but the act of man in community, the act of man and woman together. He can thereby explain the meaning of man's disobedience for the community and its effect upon it. The Yahwist then, by uniting in one the stories of man's creation and man's defection, can present an outline of a philosophy of man which embraces at the same time man's origin from God, his own personal existence, and his life in community with his fellow man. The theological, psychological, and sociological aspects of this philosophy can be summed up in the one sentence: no man can be isolated from his fellow. It is important to note, and this in opposition to the majority of the interpreters of the passage, that man is by nature and at the same time just as much a creature as he is a member of community. It is not a question of an individual who first of all is quite alone and who subsequently enters into relationship with God and into community with other individuals. From such an understanding of man it is clear that there can be theology – that is, inquiry about the relationships between God and man – only in continuing dialogue with those sciences which deal with man's understanding of himself and his social relationships. At least the following can be said: the basic questions about the relationship of God to man, of the very meaning of community and human existence, are so intertwined in the biblical reflection on Creation that they cannot be separated from each other. We can now ask how the Yahwist fitted these two narratives together, and how we can explain the construction of the narrative of the creation and transgression of man.

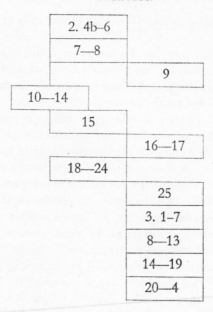

The narrative begins in 2.4b by saying that when God created man nothing existed, or what was, was not as it is today. The introductory sentence 'When ... there was not yet ...' is a common stylistic device in Creation narratives. It occurs in Egypt, in Mesopotamia and in many other places as well as in the introduction of the *Wessobrunner prayer* (one of the oldest poems of German literature, the first lines of which contain an account of Creation). This device, which serves as an introduction to a Creation narrative in so many places throughout the world, highlights something common to all reflection on Creation. It is easy then to grasp the following: every narrative must refer back to something which has gone before, to some given data. But there is nothing which has gone before the story of Creation. Creation can become the subject of a narrative only by means of a 'negative exposition', 'When ... there was not yet, then ...'. The dependent sentence comes only in v. 7: 'then the Lord God formed man ...'. The following verse, v. 8, which says that God planted a garden in Eden and put man in it, is part of the introductory action; v. 15b was added later: 'to till it and keep it'. This half-verse is for the Yahwist the point of contact between the two narratives, which coincide with each other in relating that God at the beginning put man in a garden. But whereas in the first narrative the garden is there to provide man with nourishment, in the second it is a special garden whose beauty is portrayed in v. 9 and whose trees stand in a special relationship to man (vv. 16–17). This is further underlined by the insertion between these verses of an ancient piece of information about the four rivers of Paradise and the lands which belong to them (vv. 10–14). The prohibition to eat of the fruit of a tree in this garden belongs to the second narrative (vv. 16–17). This second narrative (after the transit verse 25) is immediately continued in the scene of the seduction of the woman by the serpent (3.1–7), the trial (vv. 8–13), the punishment (vv. 14–19), and the expulsion from the garden (vv. 20–4). After the parentheses of vv. 10–14 the first narrative resumes the threads in v. 15 (15b repeats 8a) and is continued in vv. 18–24: the creature man is not precisely that which the Creator really wanted; something is not good. First of all the beasts are called upon to make up for what is still lacking. But it is only the creation of woman that brings the creation of man to its fulfilment. The narrative reaches its climax in the 'joyful welcome' (Herder) of the woman by man and closes with a typical etiological conclusion: the event which has been narrated is the foundation of something which touches the very heart of the situation of the narrator: man and woman are destined for each other and must remain together (v. 24). This is clearly the conclusion of a narrative. The short remark that both were naked and not ashamed is the preparation for the temptation scene (3.7) and forms the transit point to the second narrative. There is but one final remark to be made on this fusing together of both the narratives: they form a self-contained unit which reaches from the creation of man from the earth to the expulsion from the garden in which God has put his creature. God punishes disobedient man, who must carry the burden of existence: for the woman, the pains of childbirth; for the man, the thorns and thistles on the land he must till. At the end of the narrative the narrator refers back to the beginning: '... till you return to the ground, for out of it you were taken.' In this way the writer makes a final declaration about the nature of man: man is created from the earth and he remains bound to the earth. The earth is his field of operation and it will give him enormous possibilities for self-development. But man returns to the earth again; whatever he accomplishes, he remains bound to a course of life that reaches from birth to death.

3. The creation of man from earth

We come to the sentence 'then the Lord God formed man of dust from the ground and breathed into his nostrils the breath of life', with the philosophical reflection of one for whom the statement is quite outdated. But perhaps we ought first of all to listen a little more closely. First, we should remember that the priestly writer (1.26–31) does not say that God created man by his word. Nothing at all is said here about how the creation of man took place. The ancient idea of God creating man from the earth was clearly so widespread that it could not readily be replaced. We meet it even in the book of Job, which is certainly later than the priestly writing: 'thy hands fashioned and made me' (10.8); also '... those who dwell in houses of clay' (4.19). It occurs in many other places in the Old Testament – for example, Pss. 90.3; 103.14; 104.29; 146.4; Isa. 29.16.

The same idea occurs in Egypt, in particular in the bas-relief of the creator-god Khnum which portrays the son of the king Amenhotep III. It occurs too in the Babylonian version of the Gilgamesh epic at the creation of Enkidu:

> When Aruru heard this,
> a double of Anu she conceived within her.
> Aruru washed her hands,
> pinched off clay and cast it on the steppe.
> On the steppe she created valiant Enkidu.
> (*ANET*, ed. J. P. Pritchard, p. 74.)

But the motif is much older. It occurs in primitive cultures and is very widespread, being found in many places throughout the world. The creation of man, then, is often presented in two acts, just as in Gen. 2.7: the formation of man from clay or mud and the breathing in of the breath of life.

When one considers this very widespread and ancient motif which stretches far back into the history of the human race, one must correct the explanation which is commonly given, namely that this is something peculiar to the Yahwist in contrast to the priestly tradition and is much older. One should rather say that the Yahwist is repeating a traditional story which was current for thousands of years before him, which remained current for thousands of years after him, and which was also known at the time of the priestly writing and later. Whether he shared this presentation himself we are not able to say; but it is rather improbable. He repeats it because it is for him a 'classical' presentation which has retained its own peculiar form and force even when the manner of presentation has been changed. He uses it as a convenient tag for what he wants to say here: man receives his existence from God, and human existence is nothing else but created existence. And so this old tradition which has come down to him and which he has passed on retains an element which, for the present day psychological and anthropological reflection on the origin of man and the human race, is still quite valid: man consists of elements that belong to this earth of ours.

This takes on an additional significance when we read together with it the other sentence, that God breathed into the image he created from earth the breath of life. The vital element, life, is thereby added to the material parts of the human body. To be a living being means not just to have a soul. This is clearly shown by the following sentence: 'so man became a living being'. In Hebrew this is *nephesh hayyah*, which can be translated by 'living soul'. It does not mean that a 'living soul' is inserted into the human body; it means rather that man is created into or as a living soul, that is into a living being. And so something is said which is of basic importance for the biblical understanding of man: man, created in his state as a living being, is created as a complete unity. Any understanding of man as consisting of body and soul, or of body, soul, and spirit, is excluded from the start. When the Bible speaks of man as a creature, it means man with all that he is and in all that belongs to human existence. It does not allow for any division, anthropologically speaking, into flesh and spirit, even less for an undervaluing of the flesh and an overvaluing of the spirit. We must also consider what the author is saying by his choice of the word 'dust': 'God formed man of dust from the ground.' It occurs again at the end of the narrative in 3.19: 'you are dust and to dust you shall return'. This can only refer to man's frailty, to the fact that he is bound to a course of life which leads from birth to death. It is stated then with the utmost clarity that man, in every aspect and in every relationship of his being, remains limited, conditioned by the fact that he has been made from dust and must return to dust. It is quite proper to speak of the material side of man provided it is understood that the 'matter' is itself something created. In any case there is no sign of a philosophy of man according to which he consists of a higher and a lower part, of a corruptible body and an immortal soul. The last sentence: 'so man became a living soul [a living being]' contains something else which is important for the biblical understanding of man: man is man only in the vitality of his existence. He cannot be made an object of study apart from this vital existence. Man in the vitality of his being cannot be comprehended in an 'image of man', nor can he be made to fade into a teaching about man.

4. Man as a whole

It could well appear that all that is essential, or at least basic to the understanding of man has been said in the Creation story. That is not the case. Philosophical and theological anthropology, each in its traditional way, strives to encompass the 'essence' of man and to describe it, by isolating and making statements about what really makes man man. By way of contrast the biblical Creation narratives look at man in all his existential relationships.

This is very clear and very impressive in the Yahwist's narrative. Man is not yet man merely because he has been made. Many other things are required that man can be created as man: the means of life (v. 8), the commission to work (v. 15), community (vv. 18–24), speech (vv. 19 and 23). In the second narrative there is in addition the relationship to God and its consequences for human existence.

It is here, I think, that the biblical Creation account makes a basic – perhaps even its most important – contribution to our present-day world. As the sciences divide and subdivide and become more and more specialized, it is of some significance when a Creation narrative speaks of man and his existence in such a way as to grasp it as a whole right from its origins and so to make quite clear that subdivision and specialization must necessarily end in futility when they lose sight of the dimension of wholeness in understanding man. Note that what I have said here includes theological reflection on man – that is, theological anthropology. And theological anthropology must also end in futility if it strives to understand human existence *only* in its relationship to God; there is no man who exists merely in his relationship to God. The same goes for philosophical, psychological, and sociological anthropology in so far as any of them sets itself up as an absolute. The ever-growing subdivision and specialization of the sciences can easily lead to a conviction that each is absolutely competent. If the biblical understanding of man as presented in the Creation narratives is to be in any way effective, then it can only be in the context that all sciences which have anything at all to do with human existence as such have a common starting point, and that their inquiries must therefore eventually converge. The question arises for theology: is it really so important, in our present-day crisis of spirit, to direct all one's effort merely to setting up an isolated theological anthropology? Should not the effort be directed rather to understanding man as a whole, as expressed in the biblical reflection on the creation of man? Thereby it could bring about something quite new, namely that theological anthropology itself, in dialogue with the other sciences of man, endeavours to say something relevant to the present age and, where it can, be a help to dialogue between these same sciences.

It is only in this way that the importance of the Yahwistic Creation narrative will be seen: man, from his very origins, is concerned with providing the means of life (economics), the commission to work (the science of work, its history and its laws), community (sociology), and speech (linguistics). The author is not occupied with man as an object of theological study, but with man in all the areas of his human existence.

5. Paradise and the commission to work

A citation from a commentary will show how completely the meaning of this section can be misunderstood. The commentator wishes to establish that the commission to till and keep the garden in which God had placed man could not have belonged to the original narrative; it must be a later addition: 'Nowhere does a second hand betray itself so clearly as here. Man is in Paradise for blessed enjoyment, not to work and keep' (K. Budde, 1883).

We see here how tenaciously certain associations adhere to certain ideas. Paradise is a Persian loan word which, through the Greek translation *paradeisos*, evokes a definite image in western languages. Its basic meaning, a fenced orchard, corresponds to the word used in the Hebrew text; but the meaning which it has acquired comes from quite different sources.

The notion of a 'Paradise', a place of the blessed where peace and abundance of all goods are found, is widespread and has many different forms, one of which is typified by the description of Paradise in the Koran. It is associated with the idea of the garden of the gods which is also quite widespread, or with that of the golden age as Hesiod describes it. The 'garden in Eden', in which God puts the man he has created, is neither the one nor the other. It indicates a far-away land or an area on earth which cannot be geographically pin-pointed; it is a well-watered fertile stretch of land, very much a part of this world, where life runs its course under earthly conditions. It is a 'land of delight' (Eden), a rich and beautiful land reflecting the fact that God and man are not yet separated. It is not really a garden of God, because God has created it primarily to provide for man; but God can be close to man in the garden. It is important however that God puts man in the garden in order to till it and keep it. This means that it is no fairyland, no Utopia, no Paradise for 'blessed bliss', but that it is a land which needs tilling and care. The idea of a Paradise which is a perpetual state of bliss is quite foreign to the Old Testament. This idea belongs to an understanding of man which puts a very low value on manual labour, and which is preoccupied with the spiritual, with contemplation or mere bliss as the only thing worth striving for in life.

Work is regarded as an essential part of man's state not only in the Creation narrative but in the whole of the Old Testament. A life without work could not be a complete life; it would be an existence quite unworthy of man. And this is expressed by God putting man in the beautiful, richly watered, and fertile garden with the commission to work it; the commission gives work a meaning; the meaning is not given it by man.

The author is thinking primarily of the work of the Palestinian farmer when he uses the two verbs 'to till and to keep [watch over]'; but it would be an error to limit his meaning to this. The phrase embraces the work with which man has been commissioned and entrusted in the whole area of his life; his creative work and his work of conservation. The verbs are complementary to each other. Every human work can in some way or another share in this 'tilling and keeping'. The narrator wanted to give a basic direction to man's activity and in this way to state that it is the Creator's intention and ordinance that his creature should undertake all such work. It should be noted that man's work must be understood in this context in a functional, not in a static sense. Genesis 2 is not establishing fixed classes or states in which the work has to be performed, as for example the state of the peasant, the teaching profession, the military profession. Work must be understood functionally: God has put man into a garden; the garden and the land there need to be worked; the land is entrusted to man, who is both capable and industrious. When other types of work are demanded by a change in environment, the commission is in nowise altered. Tilling and conserving are suitably adapted. The development and specialization of work, which will be dealt with in a later passage (4.17–26), corresponds to this functional understanding of work. God's commission holds not only for definite and fixed types of work, but for work in every aspect of its development.

6. The animals

Man is now established. He has been provided with nourishment and has received a commission and thereby an occupation which gives his life meaning. But is that life? Is that really the man that God intended to create? This question is summed up in a divine reflection: 'It is not good that man be alone'. H. Gunkel remarks in his commentary at this place: 'This scene presumes a naive view of God; God makes a futile experiment. The Melanesians too tell of many unsuccessful attempts in the process of the creation of man.' Actually many primitive Creation stories are characterized by several unsuccessful attempts at creating man; only with the last attempt does the creation of man succeed. Here too material was at hand to the Yahwist; a very old motif reaching right back into the primitive cultures has been resumed. Once again the Yahwist had no need to use this idea, but he turned it to account because it enabled him to express something which was important to him. If one looks to the priestly presentation in Genesis 1, it is simply stated: '...and God created them a man and a woman [or, as man and woman].' P says nothing which is really different from what the Yahwist says. The difference is that the Yahwist takes the obvious fact of division into two sexes out of its matter-of-factness and makes it an object of critical reflection. And what is astounding is that he succeeds with an ancient, naive, and primitive manner of presentation in elevating the perfectly obvious to the level of critical consciousness. God says: 'It is not good that man should be alone'. This reflection sets solitary existence against community and states clearly that what is characteristic of being man cannot be found in mere existence as man, but that only in a community is man truly man. This is expressed in such a way that at the end of the process of creation, with man apparently complete, provided for, and taken care of, the question arises: is this good? When the answer is in the negative, then the way is open to discover hidden behind such a presentation the necessity of community for proper human existence. Something which was always there, and which everyone took for granted, is no more taken for granted; there comes an awareness of its meaning. This discovery of community and its significance for human existence can be compared, however far removed, with the rise of sociology as an independent science; here too it is being discovered that a whole range of human relationships, which had hitherto been taken for granted, is so important that it must become the object of a special science. But it strikes one as rather strange that the first attempt of the Creator to remedy this obvious lack is the creation of the animals. The possibility is raised that man might find the help which is proper to him among the animals.

The creation of the animals in ch. 2 is in a completely different context from 1.20–5. There it was a question of the animals as a part of God's created world; they were regarded as a species of living beings divided into different kinds. This corresponds to the way in which the science of zoology would put the question. The Yahwistic narrative, on the other hand, regards the animals from the point of view of their meaning for man, or what they could mean for man in the context of modern behavioural science. In Genesis 1 the creation of the animals is in the context of the creation of the world; in Genesis 2 it is in the context of the creation of man. The creation of the animals is related to man in that man, after God has formed the animals and led them to him, must himself decide whether they are that help which is proper to him. One can discern here a quite striking humanistic quality in the understanding of human relationship: God does not simply determine the sort of companion man will have; there is true community only where man accepts the companion in a free decision; man himself must say whether the partner is the right one or not.

The Gilgamesh epic provides a striking parallel to the question whether and how the beasts are related to man. The story tells that Enkidu, later the companion of Gilgamesh, is, so to speak, created in two stages: first (he too was formed from the earth), as a being that lived with the animals: 'shaggy with hair is his whole body, he is endowed with head hair like a woman.' He was like an animal in his manner of eating and drinking, he lived together with them, and they were not afraid of him. He was then seduced by a woman whom the gods had sent to him, he became familiar with the human community and a civilized man. Behind this Enkidu scene, just as behind the motif in Genesis 2.19–20, there is a tradition from a very early period, in which man stood even closer to the animal. We see once again that it was a lamentable lack of information that led to the conclusion that the biblical reflection on Creation and scientific research into the beginnings of mankind were mutually exclusive. At the time when the Creation narratives originated, people were aware that man once stood much closer to the animals; and there are traces of this awareness in the biblical story. But the biblical narrative, in contrast to the Enkidu scene, states clearly that the animals cannot be man's proper helper.

It is only when this point has been made that one can explain the positive meaning which the animals have for man. God leads the animals to man so that he can name them 'and whatever the man called every living creature, that was its name'. Here, within certain limits, man first showed his autonomy. Man must name the animals as they are; that is, as they have been created by God; man shows his own talent for the first time: he gives names to the animals and with the names the meaning which they have for him. P says, somewhat abstractly, that the Creator set man as lord over the animals (1.26–8). J says the same by narrating what took place; and he says even more clearly that dominion does not mean exploitation: man gives names to the animals and thereby gives them a function in his world. Animals as creatures have no name. They receive names only inasmuch as they are animals who have been given a function in man's world, and so it is only man himself who can give them a name. Man discovers, defines, and orders his world with the naming of the animals. It is speech that makes the world human. The animals are constituted as part of man's world by receiving names. And so it is essential that the event of name-giving begins with the animals. The older interpreters, who thought primarily of the naming of things, did not see this. Names are given primarily to living beings because they stand closest to men: what is originally named is not what exists, but what is encountered.

One must know something of the names given to the animals in the primitive languages to understand properly what this little scene means. The development from the proper name to the name of the genus is very gradual, covering a course of thousands of years. For the names of the animals this means that in many primitive languages the genus, for example the cow, has not one, but at least twelve and quite often more words to indicate that it is a cow. There was a particular description of the animal in every stage of its growth. Its every faculty had a particular description; every manifestation of its temperament, every quality of its body, received some special designation and so on. The name then expresses quite a variety of observations and experiences. The name draws together what has been collected over long generations of experience through knowledge of and encounters with the animals and their ways of life. With the giving of a name something was begun that has only been taken up again in our generation by the behavioural sciences (Konrad Lorenz); they have finally recognized once more how important for human existence is the knowledge and understanding of the animals.

I would like to add a remark and thereby to draw the attention of the behavioural sciences to an area that could be fruitful for them. In the many collections of the proverbs of primitive peoples which are now accessible to us, there is everywhere a notable proportion of comparisons with animals. These proverbs, which often have a remarkable subtlety of observation and a gentle humour, show us that, in the early stages of the history of mankind, man often tried to understand his own unique quality as man by means of pointed comparisons with the animals. They show the same intention as the Yahwistic narrator when he speaks of the meaning of the animals for the world of man.

7. Community of man and woman

'But for the man there was not found a helper fit for him.' The animals are not enough, and God creates woman. The creation of woman from the rib of the man is no more to be understood literally than the creation of man from the earth. The narrator resumes an old well-established tradition, traces of which are found in other places. He seizes on this manner of presentation because it enables him to explain from the Creation event how man and woman belong together.

Just as the Creator had already led the beasts to the man, so now he leads the woman to him, and the man receives her with 'a jubilant welcome' (J. G. Herder). She is really the helper suited to him. These two expressions bring together in essence the meaning of human community. 'Help' should not be limited in any way; it is neither help at work nor help in begetting posterity (so St Augustine). It is help in the broadest sense of the word, a mutual help in every sphere of life. To mutual help must belong mutual understanding in word and response, in silence and in activity. This simple description of human community, primarily the community of man and woman, but not only this, is surprisingly relevant; the community of man and woman in our present day can also be described in this way, despite all differences and changes in culture.

A few verses from Ecclesiastes 4.9–12 are a sort of echo of the description of community:

Two are better than one,
because they have a good reward for their toil.
For if they fall, one will lift up his fellow;
but woe to him who is alone when he falls
and has not another to lift him up.
Again, if two lie together, they are warm;
but how can one be warm alone?
And though a man might prevail against one who is alone,
two will withstand him.

The words with which the man greets the woman are rhythmic:

This is at last bone of my bones and flesh of my flesh;
she shall be called woman,
because she was taken out of man.

They are rhythmic because they repeat a cry. The cry rises
rhythmically from readily flowing speech, the speech is given
poetic form in the cry. The rhythm is not something which is
later impressed on the speech, it is rather the speech form appropriate to the cry. Such an exclamation is conditioned by the
situation; it is the expression of man's joyful surprise as he discovers in woman his companion. He cannot at this moment express himself in any way but in 'poetry' – that is, he clothes his
flow of words with the rhythm of poetic expression.

We recognize the intention of the narrator as he resumes the
two basic functions of human speech, the naming and the cry,
into the story of the creation of man. The naming, with its pre-
cision and order, refers to the scientific activity, the call to the
poetic. The basic functions of speech belong to man's becoming
man. The narrative of the creation of man reaches its climax in
the joyful exclamation with which man welcomes his companion.
The being which God has created is only now really man – man
in the community. In an appendix, v. 24, which does not belong
immediately or necessarily to the narrative, there is added an
etiological explanation of the attraction of the sexes for each
other, which brings about separation from home and parents.

The author is not so much explaining the institution of marriage; he is referring rather to the basic power of the love of man and woman, which is able to prevail in opposition to the established institutions. Something quite revolutionary is being said: the basic longing and searching for each other by those who are in love is set over against marriage which has been planned by society, conventions, and the home. The strongest bonds, even those binding one to one's parents' house, are loosed by this power. So that mysterious power, which causes two human beings to seek and to belong to each other, and which is given with and founded in the very fact of creaturehood, receives a high valuation.

If one asks finally what is being said here of the relationship of man and woman as the basic form of human relationship, then it must be emphasized that it is a question of the whole area of man's existence. It does not consist only in mutual love with its basic power of bringing two people into close union in a new community. This mutual love is put in the broader context of community of life, the essence of which is that each is so suited to the other, so corresponds to the other, that they can mutually help and live for each other. The community of man and woman in its basic outline is thereby traced right back into ancient times; and it is only what it is meant to be when it spans the whole course of human existence.

4

The Offence

The narrative which is traditionally called 'the Fall' is of such outstanding and far-reaching significance, in the Christian Church and beyond, for the understanding of man in the western civilization, that one must be extremely careful and prudent in putting the question, 'what does the text actually say?' First of all it must be stated that in the Old Testament the text did not have this all-embracing meaning. It is nowhere cited or presumed in the Old Testament; its significance is limited to the primeval events. The Old Testament knows nothing of a narrative which says that man sank into a state of corruption, that from that moment on he was 'fallen man'.

1. The command

The narrative begins with the command given to man in the garden. But before the command God leaves man perfectly free to eat from all the trees in the garden: 'God begins by allowing man complete freedom' (G. von Rad). This means that man need not suffer any want; the command does not demand any privation. What then is the meaning of the command? No explanation is given to man; one thing only is added: the command is meant to protect him from death (2.17b). The commission which man receives to till and keep the garden is utterly reasonable and intelligible; the command is not reasonable. Consequently it can only be listened to and obeyed, if he who commands is listened to and obeyed in the command. It is only when man is confident that he who commands has the good of man at heart that man will observe the command. The command therefore opens up the possibility of a relationship to him who commands. And this in fact is the real meaning of commands in the Bible. Something is entrusted to man in the command. The command introduces him to freedom; this is not the case with the animal. In the command man can put himself into a relationship with the one who commands, one way or the other.

What the priestly writing describes in abstract terms — God created man in his image, corresponding to him, so that something can happen between God and the creature — is presented here in narrative form: the possibility of something happening between God and man consists in this, that God gives man a command and man can only relate himself to this in freedom. He can abide by what has been commanded or he can reject it. In both cases he sets himself in either a positive or negative relationship to him who commands. The freedom of this relationship arises only from the command; without the command there would be no freedom.

The author wants to say that freedom belongs to the very nature of man, that in the possibility of freedom there is a broadening of man's human capabilities.

There is today a world-wide movement against all authority, and there is something in it that we cannot escape; it is meaningless to try to thrust back this development. It is all the more important then to ask, what is left of the structures of authority after the disintegration? The command in its original meaning, as intended in the Creation story, will always remain; it belongs to the nature of man. And more: it belongs to the nature of man to see himself free in face of a command and to relate himself to the one who gives the command by saying yes or no. This is quite clear in the simple forms of human relationships. When the partners in a marriage leave each other complete freedom so that each can do just as he pleases in relation to the other party, then such a marriage is senseless. The same can be said of any form of education and of any organized contract of work. The disintegration of the structures of authority can only mean that there are certain areas where authority is falling apart because of itself. Where some sort of restriction of business is demanded in certain areas, then this can only be functional – that is, it can only be based on bettering conditions of life in these areas. When the author of the Creation narratives says that it is God who is the one that gives the command, then he is saying that the command has its origin where life has its origin; but at the same time it becomes clear that there must always and everywhere be the possibility of an incomprehensible command. A command is or can be incomprehensible and consequently acceptable only in trust, where the breadth of view of the one who commands is much broader than that of the one who receives the command.

There are three basic ways in which man's conduct in community can be limited: by the taboo, the command (or prohibition), and the law. Each of these three is institutionally conditioned: the taboo is pre-personal, the command is personal, the law is post-personal. There can only be command where there is speech; the voice of him who commands must be there so as to command. There cannot be command and the consequences of command without a personal relationship to the one who issues the command. Address in the second person is inseparable from the command. The Bible offers no foundation at all for subjecting the command to the law or for describing a series of commands as law. Command is something essentially different from law.

The command in the Creation narrative has a completely positive meaning. It is an act of confidence in man in his relationship to God. It takes him seriously as man who can decide in freedom and it opens to him the possibility of loyalty.

2. The temptation, the origin of evil

This masterpiece of Old Testament narrative (3.1–7) can only be imperfectly paraphrased or repeated. The story itself says far more than any subsequent explanation can. The scene is quite self-contained. The transgression of the command could be told without it. We see then what was the intention of the narrator:

he wants to present defection as a human phenomenon. There always has been, there always will be defection. One can follow up the changing significance of defection from one area of human existence to another. The defection to other gods plays an important role in ancient Israel at the time of the entrance into the land. At certain times the defection enters into the realm of private life. In the time of the mass media the defection reaches unimagined possibilities in economic and political areas. The basic lines of the phenomenon are drawn in the Creation narrative. Man is such that under certain circumstances he can be seduced. And that is the state of any man who avails himself of this possibility. Both man's ability to defect and the intention of the one who causes him to defect point to man's limitation. That is what he is, and no ethic, no religion, no political power can alter the situation in any way.

This is the real meaning of these verses, and when, following the traditional interpretation, one sees Satan in the serpent, then this meaning is obscured. The text says nothing about this, and one thereby misses the telling point which the narrator wants to make: the serpent with its cleverness is a creature of God; God himself has created the being which leads man to disobedience. The force of this paradox must not be weakened. 'The defection . . . remains something utterly inexplicable amidst all the good that God has created. It must be left as a riddle' (W. Zimmerli). The narrator also wants to say that it is not possible to come to terms with the origin of evil. There is no etiology of the origin of evil.

This decisive point is also missed in a new mythical explanation of the serpent represented in several recent interpretations. According to this interpretation the serpent represents something magical, the beast of life or the beast of wisdom. It is said that the serpent is the symbol of Canaanite fertility cults and as such promises life (Soggin). But in this explanation the point has been missed that the primeval event is speaking of mankind and does not presuppose any division into peoples or religions. A polemic against the Canaanite fertility cult would be quite out of place here. The fact, too, that the serpent speaks is a pre-mythical motif. It occurs in fairy tales and it ought to make quite clear that the event belongs to the primeval period, to a realm on the other side of present experience.

It is a true defection. The serpent has something to offer: 'you will be like God, knowing good and evil'. There has been a long drawn out controversy about the meaning of 'the knowledge of good and evil'. The explanation is really quite simple: it means the knowledge of that which is useful or harmful to man. The expression 'the knowledge of good and evil' is an overall expression. It means knowledge in a wide sense, inasmuch as it relates to the mastery of man's existence. It proves itself in the correct judgement of what is good and what is bad, what man's existence demands and what harms it.

Only now does the real meaning of the temptation by the snake become clear. Man is created with a strong drive to live and to know. This is the root of the conflict in the relationship of man to God. Man's drive to live is limited by his life cycle, which leads to death and from which there is no way out. But the other possibility remains, to go beyond what he is with his drive after knowledge. The way seems open to him 'to be like God', and this is uncovered in the temptation. This is a temptation not because the drive towards knowledge, towards all-embracing knowledge, was of itself opposed to God; it is not, because man is created with it. But the possibility is there of a disturbance and a destruction of the proper relationship between God and man, when man in his drive after knowledge oversteps or tries to overstep his limits. The narrative of the temptation demonstrates this in an inspired manner: in transgressing God's commandment man also oversteps the limit which is his very protection in his relationship to God; when man oversteps his limits he loses his standards.

The woman saw 'that the tree was to be desired to make one wise'. This meant the same as the knowledge of good and evil in the previous verses. The woman moves outside her relationship of trust to God so as to become wise, she no longer hears in the command him who commands, who up to that very moment has carried and preserved her in existence. It is more important to her to become wise, and she transgresses the command.

The woman is led to transgress; the man does not need to be led; he simply assents. The narrator points to another way of being involved in wrongdoing: simple complicity. Another side of man is shown here; he is ready to avoid a decision, where that is possible, and allow others to decide for him. After showing the positive side of human community, the narrator now shows the negative side: the social moment of inertia, which someone has called 'community adhesiveness'. The person who goes with the current is usually a harmless type. He has neither the ability nor the energy of the seducer. He has not even the strength to stand by what is old, a strength which alone makes temptation necessary. Together with this social laziness which causes him to go along with the others, there is the laziness which prevents him from asking what the conformist will accomplish in the long run.

But the temptation has something positive to offer. Man eats the forbidden fruit and does not die. His eyes are indeed opened and he knows something which he had not known before. This section of the narrative shows a profound knowledge of man. The author sees that the transgression of a command, the overstepping of a limit which has been set for man, even when this is reprehensible and leads to death, gives man an insight which he did not have before. It is only then that the power of sin is really taken seriously.

3. The shame

They became conscious of their nakedness and they made aprons to cover themselves. At the beginning of this section we read, 'they were naked and were not ashamed' (2.25). Now they are ashamed. They have noticed something, understood something, just as the serpent had promised them. They are now in a position to do something about it. They have learnt a little more; there is no doubt about this. What is new is seen in the circumstance of shame. One interpreter (F. Delitzsch) explains: 'shame is the co-relative of sin and guilt'. And another (O. Procksch): 'the discovery of the secret of sex in the experience of shame is a consequence of sin'. But these explanations of shame are too one-sided. Shame is not something which originally affected an individual, but two together. The meaning is, they were ashamed in the presence of each other. Shame can be the reaction to a mistake. But that is not really the point. Shame is a reaction to an unmasking or a being unmasked. It is ethically ambivalent; it can occur, for example, when a person is publicly praised. This ambivalence is shown where on the one hand the lack of shame can refer to complete blamelessness (so in 2.25), whereas on the other hand 'shameless' and 'impertinence' are negative predicates. Shame can also have a positive meaning when it refers to the reaction to a false step: 'blessed the false steps, which have left shame behind in us' (G. Bernanos). It can also be effective in turning one away from sin.

The shame of man who has transgressed God's command is ambivalent. Shame indicates that man has lost something which was there before, that he has failed, that something is not right. But at the same time man knows that it is not right when he continues naked, and he is capable of supplying a remedy. Man has certainly become wise; but he has paid dearly for it with what he has lost.

4. 'Adam, where art thou?'

What man has lost only becomes clear in his meeting with God. What has happened is only uncovered as offence against God, as sin, in confrontation with God. It must be made clear that the event which is here described, a legal process and the punishment inflicted by God, was not something which actually took place. The narrator is speaking of a primeval event beyond the realm of our experience. We must ask, what does the author mean? A legal process such as this, conducted by God with the consequent punishment which God pronounces, occurs in the Old Testament only here and in the following chapter, the story of Cain and Abel. In both cases there is a consequence which comes directly from the offence itself (in ch. 4 it is the crying of the blood from the earth); only then does the personal confrontation of the process begin. With his description of the effect of a crime the narrator refers to two stages in the history of man: in an earlier stage the wicked deed of its very nature gives rise to disastrous consequences for the evil-doer, an idea which is based on the magic mentality, the 'consequential mentality' (K. Koch); reference is made here to this stage when the eating of the forbidden fruit produces an alteration in man. Then in the place of the consequential mentality there comes the personal confrontation with judgement between God and man, just as between man and man. Again we see that the reflection on Creator and Creation can embrace an understanding of development in the history of mankind. This personal legal process is presented as a trial and punishment by God.

The process begins with God appearing on the scene. It is the presupposition so that a face to face dialogue can take place. It is necessary so as to have a court process. And man hides himself from it. The court process, despite all changes and transitions, has retained something of the awesome right to the present day. Such a process is necessary where men live together in all the different forms of society hitherto known by man, and is a confirmation of how true to life the narrative is. Man is such, that this is necessary.

It is necessary to call the man by name so as to make clear to him what he has done. The order of events is reconstructed as in every legal process. The series of questions and answers shows what took place. The same is achieved here as in the prophetic literature, namely that the process according to which God punishes or judges takes place in a way that all can see. By means of the questions which are directed to the man and the woman the narrator underlines the simple basic meaning of responsibility: man has to give an answer for what he does (no question is put to the serpent). An idealistic and individualistic ethic has set conscience in the place of or above responsibility. Such a reversal of roles endangers true clarity. Conscience can

be very important for the individual and for his own understanding of himself; but the appeal to conscience is not sufficient
for maintaining the balance of order and freedom in a community. Conscience can never be substituted for responsibility.

'Conscience' is not a specifically biblical notion; it occurs only
marginally in the New Testament. It is completely lacking in
the language of the Old Testament, as in earlier languages; this
notion was only formed when individualization had developed
to a certain stage. When we say, 'You must be responsible for
that before your own conscience', then this rather remarkable
form of speech shows that responsibility can never be replaced or
superseded by conscience. Our language shows the same tendency to individualize when the real functioning of responsibility is transposed to 'a sense of responsibility'. But this can only
be secondary. Real responsibility functions just as in this narrative; a man is questioned about his conduct and must answer for
it. The question at the beginning of the passage has the same
meaning. Man hides himself, and God asks: Where are you?
But the question about man's conduct is extended to his very
being. With this simple touch the narrator says that God goes
after man who hides himself. When the trial and the punishment are introduced with this question, it is quite clear that the
whole process is being directed to the good of man and not to
his detriment. When man is called to responsibility for his conduct, he is being taken seriously as man. The Creator is taking
care of his creature when he goes after him and questions him as
he defects and hides himself. Such questioning is always implied
when the Bible speaks of God as judge. Man who is no longer
responsible is not man whom God intended.

The narrative continues this line of thought when man, confronted by God in his sin, finds that he still has one area of freedom: he can defend himself. When interpreters describe this
defence, which remains the right of the guilty, as an attempt to
fob off the guilt, then they do not come to grips with the problem. It must rather be conceded that what man alleges in his
defence is correct. The narrator with deep insight stresses that

the sin against God which he presents is very complex. The legal
process has thereby meaning because the accused can present his
view of the event. When man defends himself by daring to turn
against God – '. . . the woman whom you gave to be with me' –
then this too is truly human and an obvious method of defence.
It shows also a trace of 'the motif of divine accusation', which
plays an important role in the relationship to God in the Old
Testament. But nothing is changed; the pronouncement of guilt
and the consequent punishment cannot be avoided; it is clear,
and this is in opposition to the traditional interpretation, that it
is not a contrite sinner but a free man who stands before God as
God calls him to responsibility. And guilty man stands before
God as man in the full sense of the word; God takes guilty man
seriously in every aspect of his human existence.

The woman is then questioned and the same holds for her.
She refers back to the serpent on whom she lays the guilt. But
the serpent is not questioned. The real cause of what has happened is not made clear. The origin of evil cannot be explained.
Here we see the profound meaning of man's responsibility for
his conduct. He is responsible in the face of something which is
not explicable. He must live with the reality of evil. It can be
neither explained nor done away with. Man cannot be made
responsible for the reality of evil. Yet man is responsible for
what he does.

5. Man and his limitations

In an older form of the narrative the punishment consists exclusively in man's expulsion from the garden (vv. 20–4). This is
the only punishment proportionate to the sin. The pronouncements of punishment over the serpent, the woman, and the man
(vv. 14–19) are really by way of explanation; they merely develop
what it means for man to be driven out of the presence of God.
They are not really punishments; they simply describe the actual
state of man separated from God. The details stress above all that
human limitation, which lies at the basis of suffering, must be
acknowledged as basic for the understanding of man. An under-

standing of man that regards him only as healthy, full of dynamism, ever striving higher and advancing, is unrealistic. But it is just as unrealistic to regard him purely from the point of view of guilt and forgiveness. Suffering has always been and always will be a part of human existence. Man cannot be really understood as a creature outside the limitations of suffering and death. But when the serpent shares in the punishment, then this is an indication that man and the rest of Creation are drawn into a common relationship which is seen in the 'groaning of all creation'.

The form of the pronouncement of punishment is striking; it is formulated as a curse. Cursing is something quite different from punishment. Just as there is a distinction between an act and its consequences and a pronouncement of guilt, so there is a conscious distinction between a curse and a punishment. The narrator indicates that in the course of man's history curse preceded punishment, and he points to the different stages by the serpent being cursed but man and woman not being cursed. The curse has its origin in the magic mentality where there was not yet a sharp distinction between a thing, a beast, and a man. Later the curse was replaced by a personal and appropriate punishment. But the earlier stage of cursing is still preserved.

The pronouncement of the curse over the serpent is expressed in direct speech; this preserves the ancient form of the curse. It contains too a fragment of earlier folklore. The unusual appearance of the serpent and the way in which it moves is explained by a curse pronounced over it, just as in the second pronouncement the perpetual struggle between man and the serpent is explained. Narratives such as these, which explain the unusual qualities of animals, are found all over the world. They show a very early and intensive preoccupation with animals, which is quite pre-scientific. These narratives, despite their naivety, are a witness to an interest in the animals which is looking for points of contact between man and the rest of creatures. The narrative of Genesis 3 gives this interest a finer point: in the previous chapter (2.19-20) the author spoke of the definite place which the animals have in the world of men by virtue of their being named; here he speaks of the continual struggle between a species of animal and man, of the separation of one species of animals from others. The fact of suffering, which is here mentioned in passing, is not limited to man; it belongs to the whole of Creation.

This passing reference to the suffering of creatures was certainly misunderstood when one saw in the verse '... he will tread on your head, and you will snap at his heel' (Luther) a prophecy about Christ (or Mary), the so-called Protoevangelium. This explanation comes to grief in the interpretation of the word 'seed'; the 'seed' of man and of the serpent, between whom God has set enmity, can only refer to the succession of descendants, and not an individual. This is but one of many examples in which the zeal to interpret individual verses of the Old Testament in a christological sense has really done a great deal of damage, because attention was no longer being paid to the original meaning of the verse.

The pronouncements of punishment over the man and the woman both describe a fact of their existence which shows limitation. The author thereby succeeds in presenting man and woman as creatures, at one and the same time destined for each other by God, together with their capabilities and their limitations. He forestalls too any one-sided understanding of man which would overstress on the one hand his capabilities or on the other his limitations, as well as any understanding which could define him without regard to the difference between the sexes. These verses, it must be noted, are not really norms which lay down something for the future, but descriptions of the limitations in the very being of man and woman as they were understood at that time. Their purpose is to explain (etiologically), not to prescribe.

The pronouncement of punishment upon the woman looks to the difficulties and pains of pregnancy and childbirth, as well as to her relationship to her husband, inasmuch as her longing for him and his dominion over her stand in contrast. It is clear that no eternally valid norm is pronounced; it is a question of the lot of woman's life as it was understood at that time; we are free then to ask, to what extent does all this remain valid for us today? First we can say that it is not permissible to see here a law which prescribes pain for women in childbirth and that consequently any alleviation of pain by medical science is forbidden. That would be a dangerous misunderstanding. On the other hand it must be said just as clearly that there is something here belonging to the very being of woman, which retains its validity despite all sociological and medical change. The whole process of conception, pregnancy and birth, from the moment the child begins to be right up to its definitive separation from the mother, belongs to the life of woman.

What is said of the relationship of woman to man – 'your desire shall be for your husband' – is primarily something which belongs to the race of man and which has its basis in the bodily constitution of man and woman. But domination by man, i.e., the subjection of woman to man, is a social phenomenon which can be changed. One must pay special attention here to the distinction between the physiologically conditioned constant and the sociologically conditioned variable. This verse retains its force even when we fully accept the equality of rights of man and woman. Presuming that the pronouncements of punishment over the serpent, the woman, and the man do not lay down any norms, but intend to explain the situation which the writer faced, then the verse which says that man should be the lord of woman should not be regarded as an eternally valid norm. It describes life as it then was. And this verse cannot be alleged today as an argument against the equality of rights of man and woman. It would, however, be precipitant to set the verse aside as having nothing to say to us today. The physiological differences between man and woman will always have social effects, even when these effects are subject to change. The current effects of equality of rights have shown that. To mention but one: despite equality of rights, man still asks for woman's hand in marriage. Much more could be said. What is primary and essential is that man and woman are different and this difference must have its effects when man and woman live together with equal rights. What these verses say of the difficulty of the life of woman will have to be taken seriously in all social changes.

The pronouncement of punishment on man speaks of the difficulty of work. This also applies to the work of woman: the author is simply juxtaposing what is typical for the life of man against what is typical for the life of woman. The pronouncement has been developed; in an earlier, simpler form it would have run:

> cursed is the ground because of you;
> thorns and thistles it shall bring forth to you;
> in the sweat of your face you shall eat bread
> till you return to the ground, for out of it you were taken.

Hermann Gunkel understood these words as 'an extremely pessimistic view of human life and of agriculture', and he has had many followers. But that is not the meaning of the narrative. The intention is to describe a quite remarkable fact: that man's work is always in some way tied up with toil and effort; every area of work throws up its thorns and thistles which cannot be avoided; every worthwhile accomplishment demands sweat. Acknowledgement and acceptance of this fact have nothing at all to do with pessimism. It is sober realism which protects work from any dangerous idealizing. We must gratefully accept the progress of technology which has lightened many of man's burdens, in the factories, in the cultivation of the soil, for the housewife, and in so many other places. But this does not alter the fact that in all work which is undertaken seriously and enthusiastically, worthwhile results presume difficulty, thorns and thistles, sweat. Is there any work, be it that of the journalist, the scholar, the mechanic, or the manager, which gives real pleasure, but which has not at the same time difficulties to be faced and obstacles to be overcome?

Only when one acknowledges fully what the Bible says here of man's work, can one appreciate the commission to work of

Genesis 2.15 and be glad that labour has continued to be productive despite the thorns and thistles.

The closing words 'till you return to the ground, for out of it you were taken' do not mean that death is a punishment. They set a limit to the hardship of work. With man's return to the earth the circle of his existence, which began with his creation from earth, is closed. It is hinted here that man is more than his work, that he must not be merged in it. He is a creature in everything which falls within the circle of his existence. It is not expected of man that he will hasten towards death in a flurry of activity, but that he will lay his work aside so as to rest from it.

6. The expulsion from the garden

The real goal of the narrative is the expulsion from the garden. This is the original and the real punishment for transgressing God's command. The whole existence of man and woman is affected by this. The narrative began with God putting the creature man in the garden; it ends with man being forced to leave the garden. The narrator's intention is to span the earthly existence of man: man experiences all that being a creature means, hidden potential as well as the limits of fallibility and a life that ends in death. Man's earthly existence begins with him confronting himself where God is not, and realizing at the same time that he is a creature, that God is his Creator.

Expulsion from the garden means that man really experiences God as one who is far off. The narrative speaks of local separation; this means a real experience of the absent God in suffering and in guilt, as the Psalmist says: 'Why are you far off?' It is something like the experience of John Steinbeck's novel, *East of Eden*. The Creation narrative describes as a state something which is experienced and recognized as belonging to the essence of human existence. Two narratives, originally independent, have been welded together; and the result is that the two basic experiences of man are compressed into one story and speak with one voice – living under God's protection and blessing and being abandoned by God, the meaning and the absurdity of life and death, the Yes and the No.

The expulsion from the garden joins together two verses which give priority to life. Man gives his wife the name *Hawwah* (Eva), and the name is explained as meaning 'mother of the living'. This sentence originally belonged to the context of the birth of the first child; it is inserted here to emphasize that, despite man's disobedience and punishment, the blessing given with the act of creation remains intact. The woman receives the name 'life', a name which reflects the dignity of woman and the joy of motherhood. This joy is heard in the exultant shouts at the birth of the first child: 'I have gotten a man with the help of the Lord' (4.1). Man who is now far from God is always man blessed by God, and man's life remains open to the future just because of the power of God's blessing.

Before God leaves man to his earthly destiny, he makes garments from skins and clothes him. This concern for man precedes the expulsion from the garden. It is to be understood together with 2.25 and 3.7. Before the act of disobedience man was naked and unashamed. Afterwards his eyes were opened and he realized that he was naked. Man was capable of helping himself out and made aprons for himself. But this could not alter the fact that man was unmasked before God. At the end of the story it is God himself who clothes man. Man need no longer feel unmasked or ashamed. This is a profound way of saying that God accepts man just as he is with his weakness. It is God's will that man, just as he is, be not ashamed before his fellow man and not ashamed before God. God removes from him that constant feeling that he is a sinner; he does not wish that man be always conscious of his sins. He removes from him any sign of inferiority complex and sends him on his earthly destiny as man free and unfettered.

When man is driven from the garden he is cut off from the possibility of being like God, and that means from being creator. What is here said of the individual is said of mankind in general in the story of the Tower of Babel: mankind cannot reach to heaven, it cannot be like God. Only an indication can be given of what this means for the history of mankind. Man has always striven to go beyond himself; he will always go further. The era when, in the political field, the king was elevated to the level of God is gone forever. The era which began with the Renaissance and Humanism saw the possibility of transcendence in the cultural sphere, in outstanding intellectual accomplishment. And so arose the predicate 'creative', which was applied to the accomplishment as well as to the one responsible for it: the creative man. This predicate found almost universal acknowledgement in the field of art, until it sank to the level of 'creator of fashions' and 'creator' of hair styles. But the question remains: is a notable artistic accomplishment to be called creative, is it to be described as a creation?

At present it retreats behind the potentiality of natural science, technology, and biology. Has not man really taken over the functions of the Creator here, and does he not usurp the potentiality which hitherto had been reserved to the Creator alone?

The answer to both questions is simple and clear. Reflection on the Creator and on the work of the Creator or on creative work has meaning only where it speaks of the whole: the whole of the world and the whole of mankind. An accomplishment which is only partial, however stupendous and ingenious it may be, can never be the work of a creator or creative work. The artist who produces a work which after thousands of years loses none of its meaning, and the scientist who unleashes a power that could alter our planet Earth or the development of mankind, works with something that is already there, in the realm of something which already exists. He cannot be a creator. Any human advance in any area at all remains a human accomplishment within the limits of humanity. The really great and significant accomplishments prove this inasmuch as they are characterized by a knowledge within these limits. Every advance in the direction of what is apparently superhuman, whether it be in the field of politics, culture, science, or technology, endangers the truly human, the very fact of being a man. The Creation narrative says very clearly to the man of today, what it said when it was written: man is not there where God is, and man's potential, however it may advance, will never make him capable of being the creator.

7. The tree of life and death

Nothing has been said so far of the tree of life. It belonged to an independent narrative which was only subsequently united with the narrative of the expulsion of man from the garden. The motif of the tree of life occurs only at the end (3.22, 24) and in the introduction (2.9), where, next to the tree in the middle of the garden, 'the tree of the knowledge of good and evil', the tree of life is also mentioned. The rest of the narrative is not in any way concerned with the tree of life. The narrator could presume a knowledge of this tree on the part of his listeners, and it was his intention to remind them of the story of the tree of life. He does it by joining the conclusion of his narrative, v. 23, with another conclusion which is found in vv. 22 and 24. In this latter the reason why man is expelled from the garden is to prevent him from eating of the fruit of the tree of life. The mention of the tree of life in 2.9, where it too is introduced into the garden, has meaning only in the context of the second conclusion in vv. 22 and 24. The insertion of the motif of the tree of life is to be explained as follows: wisdom (in the sense of all-embracing knowledge) and eternal life belong to the divinity. But man is created with a longing for knowledge and with a longing for life. Striving after knowledge and after a life which is indestructible is a question of belonging to the divine; of being like God, as is presented in the temptation scene. The difference between God and man could not be more clearly expressed than in man's limitation in both areas. But there is a distinction: man can achieve the 'knowledge of good and evil' up to a certain point, even when it causes him loss rather than gain; but life indestructible is not for him; he is bounded unconditionally by death.

The tree of life was well known in ancient Israel. It occurs in Proverbs, for example ('the fruit of the righteous is the tree of life', 11.30), and in other places. It also occurs throughout the whole of the ancient East. The best-known example is the plant of life in the Gilgamesh epic (XI, 266-95):

> I will disclose, O Gilgamesh, a hidden thing,
> and a secret of the gods I will tell thee:
> this plant, like the buckthorn is . . .
> its thorns will prick thy hands just as does the rose.
> If thy hands obtain the plant, thou wilt find new life . . .
> Its name shall be 'Man Becomes Young In Old Age'.
> I myself shall eat it, and thus return to the state of my youth.

With the loss of his companion Enkidu, Gilgamesh is stricken with horror in face of the merciless fate of death and goes looking for life which is not exposed to death. Gilgamesh finds the plant of life but loses it again. He is back at the point where he was when Siduri, the ale-wife, spoke to him at the beginning of his journey (X, 3, 1-5):

> Gilgamesh, whither rovest thou?
> The life thou persuest thou shalt not find.
> When the gods created mankind,
> death for mankind they set aside,
> life in their own hands retaining.

The idea of a tree or plant or a fruit of life belongs to the realm of magic; it has its origin in the primitive cultures where there are many examples.

Access to the tree of life is forbidden, and this in the context of the narrative means that death, of which there has been a forewarning in 2.17, is an absolute condition of human existence. It is not described as a punishment for disobedience; but man alienated from God is man on the way to his death. By concluding in this way the narrator tells his hearers once more that man, notwithstanding that he has been blessed by God, that he is endowed with a life-force that is effective into the future, remains within the limits of the life-cycle allotted to him; he is forever a limited creature in the face of his Creator.

8. The Fall?

In all languages of the western world this narrative carries the title 'The Fall'. This title, which is firmly anchored in the Christian tradition of the West, implies that the narrative has a definite meaning which always accompanies it. This meaning has been established in the dogmatic theology of the Christian Church in the teaching on the original state, the fall, and original sin. This term and the meaning which it implies did not have its origin in the Christian Church and in Christian tradition; it originates in late Jewish tradition. It can be clearly seen in the fourth (second) book of Esdras (7.118):

> O Adam, what have you done?
> For though it was you who sinned,
> the fall was not yours alone,
> but ours also who are your descendants.

In this text Adam is not, as he is in the narrative itself, understood as a representative of mankind created by God, but as an historical individual whose 'Fall' was passed on through him to his descendants. The teaching of the Fall and of original sin rests on this late Jewish interpretation. It has no foundation at all in the narrative.

Paul's interpretation of Genesis 2–3, as has often been pointed out, follows the interpretation of late Judaism; it did not have its origin in Paul's encounter with Christ.

The doctrine of original sin reached its full development with Augustine. Typical of Augustine's interpretation is the following: 'man's fall is understood as a sinking to a lower level of existence, so that sin is to be understood not as a lack of something, but as a real degradation of being.' (Cf. O. Loretz, *Schöpfung und Mythus*, pp. 20–30: 'The influence of Augustine and the theological tradition on the Christian understanding on Creation'.) One can no longer say that this interpretation of Augustine, which has had such a determining influence in the Christian tradition of the West, accords with the intention of the narrator at the beginning of the Bible. This interpretation is based on the quite incorrect presupposition that our present history begins with the Fall, while the 'original state' which preceded the Fall was a state of ideal innocence quite separate from our present history. The interpretation rests on a misunderstanding; it has failed to realize that the whole course of events from man's installation in the garden to his expulsion is meant to be a primeval happening, and so something quite separate from our own history. An event in this context is presented in a quite different way from our understanding of history. The primeval story explains human existence in its essential elements from man as he actually exists. There is but one question which determines the course of the narrative: why is man, created by God, a man who is limited by death, suffering, toil, and sin? The narrative is not really answering the question of the origin of man, but the question of man experienced as ambivalent. The answer is not objective information such as man could put together in some sort of teaching. The 'message' of this narrative can only be understood by listening to it. The narrative certainly shows the connection between man's guilt and his limitation through suffering, toil, and death. But it is not said that 'the wages of sin is death'. The penalty of death, the threat which accompanies the prohibition, does not follow; man, despite his disobedience, is guaranteed the freedom of a full life. The curse does not touch man himself, but only in passing. The punishment alienates man from God, but does not mean complete separation. Guilt and death belong inseparably to man's existence, but man alienated from God always remains man whom God cares for, protects, and blesses; he remains God's creature. Only the narrative as it runs its course can say all this with all its subtlety and nuances; it cannot be compressed into a doctrine.

9. Creation of man and anthropology

The story of the creation of man and of the expulsion from the garden at the beginning of the Bible has a significance for the human race which will always be relevant.

Since the rise of the science of anthropology, and especially of the Darwinian teaching on Evolution, there has been an ever growing opposition between church teaching on original justice, the Fall, and original sin, which relies on the narrative of the creation of man, and scientific research on the beginnings of the human race. When the narrative is not speaking of two historical individuals, but of the primeval representatives of mankind, and does not mean by disobedience a determined moment in history, but a primeval happening, then this opposition becomes obsolete. May I quote a Catholic exegete in favour of this now generally accepted understanding of the Creation narrative (H. Haag, *Der „Urstand" nach dem Zeugnis der Bibel*, 1968): 'The present opinion of Catholic and Evangelical dogmatic theology, according to which the primeval state was a chronological phase at the beginning of human history ... does not accord with the Bible. The Bible knows no "sinless man" and consequently no state of innocence.' It should no longer be disputed that the phenomenon of sin and of evil has become in the course of the millennia a phenomenon affecting the whole of mankind; and that the theological dimension can no longer exclude the anthropological, psychological, and social dimensions of the explanation of this phenomenon. The significance of these sciences for the early history of man must be more and more acknowledged. I refer to the direction given to research by Sigmund Freud's depth psychology, to C. G. Jung's teaching on Archetypes, to the work of L. Housman, *Sin and Herd Instinct* (1945–6), to the work of K. Lorenz, *Das sogenannte Böse. Zur Naturgeschichte der Aggression* (1964, 3rd edn), and to O. Loretz, *Schöpfung und Mythus*, 1968. The unique and ever relevant message of the narrative of Genesis 2–3 will only become clear when the significance and necessity of scientific research into the beginnings of the human race is fully acknowledged. It is only under this pre-supposition that one can expect the science of anthropology to give fuller significance to an important reality: in the early period of human history man's development in all its dimensions is inseparable from his understanding of himself as he stands face to face with a divine power.

10. Adam and Christ

What unites the narrative of the creation of man most clearly with the account of the work of Jesus Christ in the New Testament is the universal perspective. In the latter as in the former, man is seen in the fullness of his existence beyond any constricting limits. And the message of the New Testament agrees with the presentation of the creation of man at the beginning of the Bible, in that man is seen in his state as a creature with all his potential and all his limitations through sin and death.

In the priestly Creation story, man is created in the image of God, and this means corresponding to God, so that something can happen between God and this creature. The New Testament in turn says that what happens between God and man has its centre in what is reported of Jesus of Nazareth. In the Yahwistic Creation story, what happens between God and man begins with God, by means of a command, giving man the ability to be free, to relate himself to him; and the narrative tells how man's limitation by suffering and death is in accordance with his disobedience to God and his assault on his brother. The New Testament in turn says that the same takes place in the work, preaching, suffering, and death of Jesus.

What is characteristic of the accounts of Jesus of Nazareth in the Gospels is that in his confrontations with other men, in his preaching and in his conduct, that which is basically human is completely dominant. It is a question of man in his state as a creature, man who is hungry and thirsty, who is sick and healthy, man in his basic community structures, man who asks about the meaning of life, about the meaning of fulfilment. And in the work which Jesus knows has been destined for him by his father, it is a question of the limitations of human existence, just as in the narrative of the creation of man: it concerns man's fallibility, his suffering and death.

Jesus of Nazareth and his disciples stand then in the middle of the tradition and history of their people. His work is directed primarily to his people; he belongs to them and he works in the midst of them and for them. But from the beginning of his work to its very end he is destined for man in his state as a creature, in the basic qualities of his human existence, as the Creation narrative presents him.

The connections between the story of the creation of man and what the Gospels narrate of Jesus of Nazareth are self-evident; there is no need for any systematization or any theological cerebration. It is perfectly obvious that man presented in the Creation narratives is man who meets us in the Gospels; that the history of the relationship between God and man of the Creation story is what the Gospels are talking about.

5

Creation and Redemption

When we discuss Creation and redemption, a natural starting point suggests itself, the Apostles' Creed; here both are spoken of in a proper and normative way. The Creed draws together the work of the Creator, the work of Jesus Christ, and the work of the Holy Spirit. This summary contains what is basic and common to all Christian Churches. It has become a matter of course for all the Christian Churches to start from this basis when they draw together this threefold work of God under a formula of belief. But when man inquires about the biblical basis, then it is no longer quite so obvious. It becomes clear that the biblical reflection on Creation cannot be comprehended under a formula of belief in the same way as the reflection on redemption. If one examines the New Testament and the Old Testament more closely, one comes across the surprising fact that the verb 'believe' is never used in relation to the Creator or in the context of reflection on Creation.

1. We must here put two questions: why is it that in the Old Testament the words 'creator' and 'creation' are never used in the context of believing? And what is meant by resuming God's creative work under the notion of belief?

To the first question: the Old Testament notion of belief presumes the possibility of an alternative, just as we do in our everyday and secular use of the word. We ask, do you believe that or do you not? In the oldest layers of the New Testament the verb 'believe' occurs mostly with a negative meaning – that is, belief is prominent where someone does not believe. In the Old Testament an alternative to belief in Creation or Creator is quite unthinkable. The creation of the world is not an object of belief, but a presupposition for thought. God's saving action can be an object of belief; Creation cannot.

To the second question: when God's creative activity is brought under the notion of belief, there is of necessity a marked closing of the gap between Creation and redemption. Creation is then something in which man can believe or not believe; it is an object of belief in the same sense as redemption. But here there is the danger of a far-reaching and quite unconscious distortion of what the Bible means with its reflection on Creator and Creation. Another approach raises the same problem. Creation is in this way subordinated not only to the notion of belief but also to the notion of revelation. One speaks of a revelation of Creation, corresponding to a revelation of salvation – or, to put it more abstractly, of a general revelation and a special revelation. A whole succession of theological discussions has arisen with the question, if and how God reveals himself through Creation or through nature. One can support this distinction by what Paul has to say in the letter to the Romans. The situation is quite different in the Old Testament. There, Creation is never the object of a revelation and it is never in any way brought into the context of revelation. We speak today, as if it were quite obvious, of the biblical witness to Creation. But that is an inexact way of speaking, because in this way Creation is made to be something which of its very nature it cannot be. There was no witness at Creation. Accordingly there cannot be a witness in any sense to the fact of Creation.

2. A few remarks must now be made about the words 'creation' and 'redemption'. In the priestly account of Creation there is a special word for God's creative act: *bara'*, a specifically theological word. It is of the utmost significance that this word *bara'* occurs in the Old Testament only with God as its subject; it never has a man for subject. And never is there any material named out of which God creates the world. Now too much has

been read into the notion behind this word *bara'*, and it has been said that the biblical theology of Creation is contained in the notion behind *bara'*. This is an exaggeration; and the exaggeration becomes obvious when we see that the priestly writing also uses the simple word 'make' in the same sense. What is peculiar to the Creation faith cannot be compassed in a mere word. The priestly writing, in its reflection on Creation, resumes more ancient and more primitive layers of tradition which spoke simply of 'making' or 'forming'. The priestly writer subsumes rather than rejects this primitive manner of speaking. The same holds for the . priestly presentation of Creation as a whole. It is formed from two layers; only the more recent layer is familiar with Creation through the word; the older layer, which speaks of God making or separating or forming, is taken up into the presentation of Creation through God's word. The conclusion is that the Old Testament did not limit itself to one definite way of presenting Creation which was the only correct one, but allowed different ways of presentation to stand side by side.

And now to the notion of redemption. In English (as well as in German) the word 'redemption' has a religious meaning. The word has passed over from the realm of religious language to the secular, so that one can say in secular language: I feel that I have been redeemed (released). But the religious echo cannot be removed from this word. It is a specifically religious word. The idea of redemption goes back to the basic Old Testament notions of saving, separating, freeing, and releasing. These words have no specifically religious meaning, but they repeat the human experience of saving, independent of who the saviour is. The English (and German) notion of redemption follows the long tradition of the word in the language of the Greek New Testament and of the Septuagint.

The Latin Bible used the word *salus* to render the Greek *soteria*. *Salus* is something different from *soteria*. The German word *Heil* (redemption, happiness, blessedness) corresponds to the Latin *salus*. The sense of the Latin *salus* is seen best in its use in greetings, just as in the Romance languages. The Hebrew equivalent for *salus* is not a word which means 'saving'; it is *shalom*, a word which expresses a state of well-being, especially the well-being of a community. A complete change has taken place here. Our notion of salvation, even in the context of experience of salvation or of salvation history, relies on a word that is scarcely the equivalent of the Greek *soteria*, and not at all the equivalent of the Hebrew word which is behind *soteria*. The word salvation has come to mean a state instead of an act, a saving or a redeeming. This idea of a state belongs originally to the context of God's act of blessing rather than of his act of saving.

Redempt

3. What then is the relationship between creation and salvation, between God's creative act and God's saving act in the Bible? The Apostles' Creed, which is our starting point, brings together three basic acts of God: creation, saving in Christ, and the action of the Holy Spirit. And it does so in such a way as to bring all three acts of God under the act of faith. This Christian Credo has its forerunner in the Old Testament, in what is called the historical Credo, as G. von Rad has demonstrated. In this historical Credo Israel acknowledges God's saving act at the beginning. These saving acts of God begin with the event of the Exodus and at times point to what happened previously in the period of the Patriarchs. But God's creative action does not occur in this Credo.

(*a*) What is the reason for this? We ask first: is there no place in the Old Testament where these two notions are brought together? Yes, in the praise of God in the Psalms. In the praise of God everything that God does is focused on one point. That is clear in Psalm 113. The Psalm begins with a call to praise God: 'Praise the Lord! Praise, O servants of the Lord, praise the name of the Lord.' In the middle of the Psalm comes the verse: 'who is like the Lord our God who is seated on high, who looks far down upon the heavens and the earth?' Israel expresses her praise of God in the polarity of God's majesty and his penetration down into the deep. God looks down into the deep in order to raise up from the deep; from man's point of view this raising up means salvation. This basic cry of the praise of God is continued into the New Testament, especially in the Magnificat at the beginning of the Gospel of Luke. When one side of this polarity is developed, 'he who is enthroned above', this usually occurs in two phrases: God's majesty is shown by the fact that he is both the Creator and the Lord of history. This is the case in Psalm 33. That is to say, there is a relationship of polarity between what the Psalmist says of God as saviour and redeemer, and of God as Creator. It can only be presented by the one being set against the other: by unfolding God's majesty in such a way as to speak of the Creator. It is essential for understanding the Old Testament that the relationship between Creation and redemption consists in a polarity. The attempt is nowhere made to bring both under the one notion. And so there is no all-embracing notion of revelation or belief. One must speak of them side by side. They cannot be brought under the one label; or, in other words, what is common to Creation and redemption is not a notion of belief or of revelation; it is God himself. The work of the Creator both in the Old and in the New Testament has its own setting; it has a different origin and history from the work of the saviour.

(b) Let us start now from the New Testament. When the New Testament speaks of the Creator, it presumes a tradition. The New Testament could not speak of the Creator unless its writers already had a knowledge of what is meant by the Creator. When the New Testament speaks of the Creator it is usually in a parenthesis. There are no notable passages in the New Testament which deal with the Creator as such. The New Testament writers are conscious that they speak as heirs of a tradition in these places. They received reflection on the Creator as part of their inheritance and tried, each in his own way, to set it in a new context. An example is Paul in the letter to the Romans. John did this in a quite different way in the prologue to his Gospel; he assumed a traditional manner of reflection on the Creator into a new reflection. It was different again in the letter to the Hebrews, and again in the letter to the Colossians. Tradition and interpretation determine reflection on the Creator in the New Testament. The question is: why must the New Testament speak at all of the Creator? This is the basic question which the Marcionites asked. And the answer was given: no, our God, the father of Jesus Christ, is not the Creator. From that point onwards Christian teaching about the Creator took its stand in opposition to the Marcionites. But it was necessary for the history of the Church that the Marcionites put this question; someone had to put it. Reflection on the Creator is not based on Christian reflection as such. That had to be seen once and for all. Only then did it become clear that one cannot speak of Jesus Christ without speaking of the Creator. And that has remained the case right up to the present day. Today radical attempts are again being made to eliminate reflection on the Creation from Christian reflection. Once more the Christian Church is asked, why does she maintain that God is the Creator? And the question demands a basic rethinking of the matter. We can state first: reflection on the Creator in the New Testament is something which has been handed on; but it is precisely as something handed on that it is necessary for the New Testament message on salvation. Just because salvation in Christ was for the whole world and the whole of mankind, it must be linked with the Creator of the world and with mankind.

There is no difference in the Old Testament. Reflection on the Creator was not something created within the circle of the Old Testament tradition itself. When the Old Testament writers speak of the Creator they are just as much heirs as are the New Testament writers. Reflection on the Creator in the Old Testament is certainly incomparably richer and more varied; but today we can no longer pass by the fact that it is the reflection of those who have inherited, of those who have received, who have received and interpreted just as has the author of the prologue of John's Gospel. It was in the middle of the last century that the religious parallels to Genesis 1 first became known, especially the Babylonian story of Creation in the epic *Enuma Elish*, in which there is a certain passage which bears a remarkable resemblance to the Creation story of Genesis 1. Immediately the interpreters of the Old Testament, Jewish, Catholic, and Evangelical alike, took a predominantly apologetic stand; their intention was to demonstrate that the biblical accounts of Creation were quite unique and incomparably superior to all parallels. But this defensive attitude does not do justice to the problem. Today we are aware that the men who wrote these imposing chapters of the Bible knew they were heirs, and that they did not wish to create something which we would call original; we know that, in their reflection on the primeval events, they were deeply concerned to throw up a bridge between what others had been saying for thousands of years and their belief in Yahweh alone. The breathtaking skill of the biblical primeval story consists precisely in throwing up this bridge. The older, Yahwistic, account of Creation says that God formed man from earth or clay. An earlier stage of interpretation thought that when this was said, it was said as a revelation of God for the people. We know today that the creation of man from clay or earth goes back beyond the Babylonian and Egyptian accounts into the primitive religions, and occurs in many places throughout the world. The biblical account is saying nothing new or nothing unique. Those who said it and those who heard it knew it, and did not hear it as if it were a new revelation from God. This holds not only for a primitive account of the creation of man from clay; it holds just as much for the creation of man in the image of God. Creation in the image of God occurs both in Mesopotamia and in Egypt. And more, it is one of those motifs which goes back to the primitive religions. The meaning of the reflection on the creation of man in the image of God becomes clear in the background of this prehistory. It is not a quality of man, it is not his spiritual nature, his personality, or his upright stance; it is human existence as such. God created man to correspond to him, to stand before him.

A further important modification of the current view must be made. The Creation stories had hitherto been traced back to man's intellectual inquiry about the origin of the world, of life, and of mankind. But these narratives had their origin in man's concern about his life in the world. The stories of the origins are concerned with the subsistence of the world and of mankind, not with the intellectual question of the origin.

Speaking out of such a vast background, we must say the Bible has much in common with very many religions in its reflection on the primeval events; the question naturally follows, is there anything special in the biblical account? I think that in this way we will be able to overcome the defensive attitude. Scholars in many branches of research, historians of religion, ethnologists, theologians, and others, have made the suprising discovery that reflection on the primeval era of mankind is not characterized by limitless variety, with the result that there are endless possibilities of presenting the origins of things; on the contrary, these are surprisingly meagre. The types of Creation account are not without limit; rather there are a few basic forms with variations, which can be quite easily understood throughout the whole world. And consequently, what is special in the biblical account can be seen more clearly than before. In our Christian dogmatic theology the account of the Fall is inseparably tied to the story of primeval times. Accordingly the biblical account of the origins has been limited to Genesis 1–3, to the account of Creation and the account of the Fall. There has not been a word on what follows in chs. 4–11, which contain an essential part of the account, namely the genealogies. Through the literary form of genealogies the authors are saying that the power of the blessing which God gave to man when he created him continues effectively. There is a direct point of contact between the story of Creation and the genealogies, which lead from Adam to Abraham. And further: it is misleading to speak of the story of the Fall. The title 'Fall', which goes back to late Jewish interpretation, suggests that man was created on a definite plane, that through the sin of one individual the whole of mankind, so to speak, 'fell' to a lower plane, and that all subsequent history was played out on this lower plane right up to the time of Christ. But this is to deal rough-handedly with the biblical data. The account of the origins shows in great depth and with great clarity that it belongs to man's very state as a creature that he is defective. And this defectiveness does not show itself in one single act in history, but in a variety of ways. The Yahwistic account of the origins expresses this by showing how man defects in different ways. Basic is the transgression of God's command which leads to man's expulsion from God's garden. This defectiveness includes the human potential to murder one of his own species, a trait which distinguishes man from the animals which do not kill members of their own (Genesis 4). God allows mankind to continue living beyond him who kills his brother. A quite different form of man's defectiveness is seen in the story of the Tower of Babel – the overstepping of limits. A whole series of accounts of man overstepping his limits is presented in Genesis 1–11. What is peculiar to the biblical treatment of sin in the account of the origins is man's many-sided defectiveness and sinfulness. Man estranged from God by his defections and transgressions is not, however, deprived of God's effective blessing. The blessing given at creation perseveres and shows its effectiveness in the succession of generations.

(c) The activity of God who saves forms the centre of the Old Testament just as of the New. The message of salvation in Christ stands in the middle of the New Testament; the confession of Israel's salvation at the beginning stands in the middle of the Old. The relationship between salvation and Creation in the Old Testament can be seen most clearly in the construction of the Pentateuch. In the middle of the Pentateuch stands God's saving action towards his people as he leads them out of Egypt. The whole is centred around this event. This centre-piece is then developed by the history of the patriarchs, which shows what sort of a people they were before this time, right back to the story of the origins. The account of God's saving action is the middle. But this saving action of God cannot be told without basing it on what has gone before; and this is extended back to the very beginnings of mankind. What happened to Israel did not happen to Israel alone; God was concerned with the whole of mankind. All then is traced back to the very beginning. There is then a coherence; God's saving action, the *soteria*, is an event which varies in the course of history. God led Israel in such a way that she praised him as her saviour and based her relationship to him on the saving act at the beginning. But God's saving act is not understood merely as something in the past; it is always going on. The greatest danger to Israel lay in the areas of politics and simple human existence. On her way through the desert Israel saw herself threatened by the forces of nature with hunger and thirst, and threatened at the same time by enemies. When she came into the land, she was threatened by political powers. Later the real threat to Israel was quite different; she was threatened with falling away from her God. This is one of the most far-reaching changes in Israel's history with God: danger from outside was replaced by danger within; Israel herself could fall away from her God. It is here that the prophets enter. They enter where the real danger to the people has become the danger of apostasy. Salvation can no longer be effected by the destruction of Israel's enemies, but only by Israel turning back to her God. This is the reason why the second Isaiah's idea of salvation – salvation as a leading home – is based on forgiveness. Salvation based on forgiveness does not occur for the first time in the New Testament; it is already found in 2 Isaiah and is preached by him. It is this same prophet who binds firmly together Creation and redemption. In his promise that they will return home he directs the gaze of the helpless remnant of his people in exile to the majesty of the Creator: 'Have you not known? Have you not heard? the Lord is the everlasting God, the creator of the ends of the earth. He does not faint or grow weary . . .' (Isa. 40. 12–31).

This same polarity of Creation and redemption appears too in the work of Jesus, as is clear from the construction of the Gospels. The Gospels are not merely an introduction to the story of the Passion. What Jesus does in the first part of the Gospels corresponds to God's work of blessing. Jesus is the healer in the quite simple sense that he heals and restores again what God has created and put into the world, by giving help to the sick, by feeding the hungry, and by rescuing men who are in danger of death. The same message is found in the mission of the disciples in Matt. ch. 10. Jesus sends out his disciples not only with a message but also with a blessing. And it is the same in the Acts of the Apostles. The Acts narrate not only a history of the Christian message but, at the same time, the progress of the blessing. The God who guides and protects the messengers of Jesus Christ on their way, and gives them the right word at the right time, is the same God who guides and protects Abraham's servant in Genesis ch. 24 and gives him the right word at the right time. I would refer finally to the Apocalyptic writings. There is a correspondence between the Apocalyptic writings and the same universality which characterizes the reflection on Creation and the primeval period. At the end, the Apocalyptic writings are concerned not merely with the fate of the community or with the fate of the Christian faith, but with the fate of the whole world, just as the first eleven chapters of Genesis are concerned with the fate of the whole world in the context of God's action of creation and blessing.

The polarity of Creation and redemption can be traced through the whole Bible, Old and New Testaments. Their relationship to each other is extremely varied. They cannot be constrained under the one notion, but neither can they be separated from each other.